The World of Jo Davidson

THE WORLD OF
JO DAVIDSON

by Lois Harris Kuhn

ILLUSTRATED BY LEONARD EVERETT FISHER

FARRAR, STRAUS AND CUDAHY

JEWISH PUBLICATION SOCIETY

Contents

Author's Note

Much of the material for this book on Jo Davidson was furnished from original sources, specifically Jo's autobiography, *Between Sittings*, Dial Press, New York, 1951, and the fond memories, letters, photographs, and conversations of Florence Lucius Davidson.

In addition, magazines such as *Time, Newsweek, The Saturday Review of Literature*, the *New York Times Sunday Magazine* section, as well as the regular newspaper editions of the *Times*, and other newspapers were used.

The Library of the Metropolitan Museum of Art in New York City allowed their files on Jo Davidson's exhibitions to be examined.

Material for the chapters on Helen Keller was graciously released by Mr. Van Wyck Brooks, who generously permitted use of material from his books which would help make this biography of his friend, Jo Davidson, possible. Books used in this measure were *Helen Keller, Sketch for a Portrait*, Dutton, New York, 1955, and *Our Literary Heritage: A Pictorial History of the Writer in America*, Dutton, New York, 1956.

The recollections and snapshots of Mr. Angelo Frudakis—mementos of days he spent with Jo—helped form some of the background material.

In addition, I wish to thank Mr. Gorham Munson and Mr. Charles Angoff for their encouragement, Paul and Marc Kuhn for giving up so much of their playtime to listen to their mother's raw material, and the many friends who definitely helped make this book a reality.

Most of all, this book has been drawn upon my own recollections as a viewer at Jo's exhibitions, where I learned in a single instant that history can be beautiful as well as exciting. And more, that a fine artist can *make* history!

JO DAVIDSON

1883-1952

In the Talmud it is written that God took dust from the center of the earth, and from all quarters thereof, and He mingled it with the waters of all the seas to create man. . . .

So Jo Davidson, sculptor, used God's own materials to re-create men and women—men and women who came from the center of the earth, and from all the quarters thereof, and from all the seas, for Jo knew instinctively, even as Malachi, the prophet, had known and asked, "Hath we not all one Father? Hath not one God created us all?"

The World of Jo Davidson

1. House of Neckties

It was a fine spring day and the boys were having a game of ball in the streets. That was where you played if you lived in New York's lower East side. Just at the moment when the game was at its best, one of the mothers spoiled it!

"Jo-eey!" she called. "Jo-eey! Come in the house this instant!"

Jo-eey heard her, but he didn't move. He let her call again.

"Jo-eey! Jo-eey!"

Darn it, he thought. Always calling me just when the game's going good. Besides, that "Jo-*eey*" sounds funny. There's something about it I don't like.

His mother called a third time. "Jo-eey! I know you hear me. Now, come in! You hear? Jo-eey!"

He threw down his glove, waved "So-long" to the gang and marched upstairs to the small flat where he lived with his parents and three older sisters. His mother met him at the door.

"You heard me call, didn't you? So why didn't you come right away?"

He looked at her intently and made up his mind. He was only a young boy, but he had certain strong feelings about things, even then. He dearly loved his mother, but she must stop that business of calling him "Jo-*eey*." So must everyone else.

"From now on," he said, his dark eyes glowing, "I want you to call me Jo!"

"Jo?"

"Yes. Just Jo. That's my name. Jo Davidson! You call me that, Mother, and I'll come right away!"

From then on, his mother did call him Jo. Jo Davidson. So did everyone he knew—even some of the most important people in the world. He was that kind of boy. He was that kind of man.

Even in the beginning of growing up, he had a sure sense of what a sculptor should have sense about. He knew instinctively where to begin, what to leave out, and when to stop. It was the same sort of feeling he had about his name. Because of this knowledge, he was to become one of the world's greatest sculptors.

Jo Davidson was born in New York City in 1883. That was the year Buffalo Bill opened his Wild West show with the famous girl sharpshooter, Annie Oakley. There were thirty-nine states in the Union and, therefore, thirty-nine stars in the United States flag. Brooklyn Bridge, which had only been a drawing on the engineer's board in 1870, was at last, after thirteen long years, finished and ready for use. Thousands upon thousands of boys and girls in New York City worked in factories. The Children's Aid Society supported schools for them to attend at night so that they could learn how to read and write—if they weren't too tired to do so. People rode in horse-drawn carriages, and J. Pierpont Morgan, one of the richest men in the country, had the first private home in New York City to be lit by electricity. In Italy, that year, another baby was born. His name was Benito Mussolini. He would play a tremendous, though ugly, role in the history of the world Jo Davidson knew. It was a period of moving, sweeping changes.

Jo's father, Jacob Davidson, was a deeply religious man, a Russian Jew, one of the more than two million immigrants who arrived in New York between 1880 and 1884. He was the father of three girls, Nancy, Rachie (short for Rachael), and Rose. But he had no son! More than anything else in the world, Jacob Davidson yearned for a son. It seemed to him that when Jo was born, all his prayers had been answered.

No one was ever to know for certain what it was that Jacob Davidson thought having a son meant. Whatever it was, it was obvious—almost right away— that Jo was unlike anyone his father had expected. In fact, Jo was like no one else. He asked far too many questions. He made pictures of everything he saw. He was so filled with life and laughter that everyone around him responded to it. Everybody—everything —small or large—interested Jo! It was a good thing for the boy that his mother, Haya, understood him completely.

Haya Davidson was an amazing woman. She seldom had money enough to take care of her children properly, yet somehow she always found a way. Food would be made to stretch in order that she could feed her youngsters, and still have a tidbit for chance guests!

Haya was wise in other ways as well, in ways more important, perhaps, than stretching a budget. She could tell stories, all kinds of stories. She realized that often a story can make people forget their troubles. When dinner was scanty—as it often was, then Haya would tell her children the tales she knew. Sometimes she spoke about growing up in Russia, sometimes the stories were about relatives and friends. Whatever she told, Jo couldn't get enough.

In addition, Haya designed and made neckties. She cut them out and Jo's three sisters would press them, for by now Jacob Davidson was so frequently wrapped up in his books that he kept forgetting that this is a world where there is rent to pay, shoes to buy, and food to be eaten. As a child, it sometimes seemed to Jo that he lived in a house of neckties. They hung from clotheslines in the living room, kitchen, and hallway. They were often found in the bedrooms.

He never completely understood why his mother had to make neckties, but he found that the busier his mother was with them, the more of life's small comforts the family seemed to have. The hamburger was more meat and less bread. Sometimes there were even extra bagels. What he always understood was the way his mother talked and how she said things. He felt that his mother used words the way no one else ever did. She glowed when she spoke—almost as if something deep down inside her spilled out and lighted up the words. If only he had such a gift!

As Jo grew into manhood and fame, it was his words, his way of using them that made him able to talk to the people who came to him. Then he could get them to relax so that he could "catch" them as they actually were. His mother's gift turned out to be his as well. He would keep talking, asking questions, and sooner or later his models acted as they did only when they were most completely themselves. Then—just at *that* instant, Jo "captured" them!

2. The Magic of Words

Signposts along the way act as a guide for the traveler. Looking over the course of Jo's life, from the beginning, we have already seen two—the changing of his name and the gift of words. There were other signposts as well.

First, there was the horse. Jo had very few toys and one day someone gave him a toy horse. It was a rocking horse and the feet were fastened to a board which had wheels. He only had the toy for a day or so when his mother found him taking it apart.

"Jo Davidson!" she said with anger. "How dare you destroy such a fine toy! What kind of boy are you anyway?"

Jo looked up, astonished. "But you don't understand, Mother. I'm not destroying it. I'm only taking off the wheels and the board so the horse will be a *real* one."

"How will that make it better? It was made to ride just the way it is!"

"But that's it, Mother! Don't you see? A real, true horse always stands on its *own* four legs. If I take off the board and wheels, this one can too! His legs are fine and strong and I can play with him much better if he's almost like the real thing."

In this manner Jo rode the horse and pretended he was riding for the Pony Express, or was a hero in the Civil War leading his troops to victory. Sometimes, he was Buffalo Bill himself! And always, the horse was there beneath him, sturdy and solid on its own four legs, as near the real thing as Jo could make him!

He had so much fun riding that horse that his sisters wanted to ride too. Usually, they pretended to be

Annie Oakley or one of those wonderful pioneer women who wasn't the least bit afraid of anything in the world. At the time, Jo's sisters were all much heavier than he was, but Jo didn't think about that. The toy horse was crushed under the extra weight. Jo never forgot it!

Years and years later, when he was a man well past the middle years of his life, the memory of that toy was fresh in his mind. Out of a childhood of hunger and struggle, that broken toy represented one of his greatest sorrows.

"Jo Davidson! Now what are you doing?" his teacher would ask. "I no sooner finish scolding you about drawing than you do it again! This is supposed to be our arithmetic period."

Jo lowered his head, embarrassed. "I'm sorry. I did do the first three problems, but then I began to watch you at the blackboard and I couldn't help drawing."

Sadly, he presented his arithmetic paper to his upset teacher. Three sums, correctly solved, were written on it, but beneath these was the best picture the teacher had ever seen of herself! How long could anyone stay angry with such a boy?

"Here's another piece of paper, Jo," she'd say then, still wondering at the child's talent. "Finish your sums. Next week we're going to celebrate Abraham Lincoln's birthday. If you try hard all this week to draw only during art class, you may make a design with colored chalk on the blackboard for Lincoln's birthday."

When the day came, Jo was ready. Whenever he drew anything on the blackboard, however, he made certain there was an American flag and the eagle, bright in their colors. Jo loved his country, loved everything it represented or that represented it. Although he was to travel thousands of miles during his lifetime, live abroad, and do busts of many people—some of whom he didn't even like, the United States always had one of its best ambassadors in Jo. He represented sincerely all the enthusiasm and courage of the ideal that is America.

Now Jo was twelve and grammar school was almost over for him. He would have liked to stop right then. Money was badly needed at home. He wanted to find a job so his mother could stop working so hard. After all, he was almost a man, wasn't he? But his mother and sisters insisted on his completing the eighth grade, at least.

"But I can go to school at night!" he protested. "And in the day time I can work and earn money to help."

"There's time enough for that when you finish school," his mother said. "Why you're still a young boy—you haven't had bar-mitzvah yet."

Jo finished that last year in grammar school.

By the time Jo received bar-mitzvah, still dreaming of a life in which he did nothing but draw and draw, all day long, many new things were continuing to happen in the world. Some of them Jo knew about, even then. In his own community, George Eastman's Kodak cameras were beginning to be known and used everywhere. Someday, such cameras would be used to show Jo's fine work. A boy named Franklin Delano Roosevelt, who lived in the same state as Jo, finished celebrating his fourteenth birthday just as Jo was getting ready for the celebration of his thirteenth in the synagogue. If you had asked Jo about this boy then, he wouldn't have been at all interested. After all, what had it to do with him? For that matter, if you had asked the Roosevelt boy about Jo, he wouldn't have cared either. Yet one day, there would be a close relationship between them! Another little boy, Dwight David Eisenhower, was entering first grade that year, but all these youngsters were so far apart, how could they possibly mean anything to one another?

Jo had finished grade school and was working now. Jobs were not too plentiful, yet he always managed to find something. He never cared whether the work was hard or long. He sold newspapers, ran errands, was an apprentice to a housepainter. Sometimes he worked from seven in the morning to seven at night. All the while he worked, no matter what he did or where he was, he thought about drawing. He had the same kind of hunger for it that he had for food. His sister, Rachie, seemed to understand that more than anyone else.

At night, he attended evening classes, and in addition, he managed each week to lay aside three cents—the price then for the art course he took at the Educational Alliance, which was the community center for Jewish life in East Side New York.

Sometimes on the way to the Alliance, Jo passed a candy store. He always stopped to peer at the jars filled with large colored gumdrops, licorice strips, mint leaves, Mary Janes, Turkish taffy, caramels, and orange slices. Ten cents would buy an enormous amount of candy in those days. Three cents alone purchased a huge bag! He would stare and stare into the window, pressing his bright young face against it, then suddenly find himself *in* the store.

"Well, young fellow, what's it going to be?" the candy store man would ask.

"I'll have a penny's worth of chocolate rabbits and a penny's worth of peanut brittle, and a jaw breaker, and—" Jo stopped. "I'm sorry, mister, but I—I can't buy them. I didn't mean to make any trouble, honest."

"Now, now, make up your mind, son!" The man had already reached for a bag and begun to fill it with the five small chocolate pieces one bought for a penny. "No money?" The owner of the store was curious, for there was Jo looking right at the three cents held in the palm of his hand.

Jo shook his head regretfully. "It isn't that, sir. I have money all right, only I need it for something more important than candy."

He put the pennies in his pocket and began to walk quickly out of the store. When he reached the door, the man called him back.

"Come here, young feller! I want to know—what is it that's more important to a boy than candy? What do you expect to do with that three cents?"

"It's my art lesson money. Someday I'm going to be a great artist."

"How do you know?"

"I just do, that's all."

"Nobody ever knows what he's going to be when he grows up. Now take me—I was going to be a fireman. In charge of the hook and ladder. Ride in a shiny, red wagon with the fastest horses in town. Here I am, running a candy store!"

"I *am* going to be an artist!"

The store owner looked at him, then held out the bag with the chocolate bunnies Jo had started to buy.

"You know, son, maybe you're right at that. Maybe you'll be a real good artist, the best there is! Here—take the candy. It's on the house!"

And Jo, having thanked the man, happily munched

his chocolate, saving one for after class to take home to Rachie. All the way to school, he thought of the kindness of this stranger. People everywhere, he thought, all sorts of people, were so wonderful!

Jo kept getting and losing jobs—always for the same reason. He didn't mean to do badly at work, but as soon as he had a spare moment, he forgot about the job and began to draw.

Once he worked for Western Union. There he drew some of the boys with whom he worked. One of them suggested Jo try to get a job on a newspaper. In those days, photographs had not yet come into general use in newspapers and all illustrations were drawn by hand. Jo immediately got a job on one of the papers, hoping to learn more about art by watching the top artist for the paper draw pictures for the front page articles.

"What a fine drawing!" Jo said to the artist who was sketching the head of the famous French writer, Anatole France. "If only I could do that well!"

"It isn't every day an artist has a chance to draw a face like this one! Anatole France is more than a world-famous author—he's a fine man and his face shows it."

"He does look wonderful," Jo acknowledged. "But your drawing is wonderful too!"

Beyond that, Jo never gave Anatole France another thought. Why should he?

Across the Pacific that year, a baby girl was born. Her name was Mei-ling Soong. When she grew up, famous in her own right, she married General Chiang Kai-shek. Right now, she was only another baby, born in a far off place. Jo knew nothing about her birth and if he had, he would not have thought it mattered to him.

Yet though the distance was great between all these people, almost beyond Jo's imagination, someday they would meet! The pattern was already clear, though none of them knew it. Each signpost was in place. Jo was well on his journey, but the time and opportunity were of God's making.

So the Bible tells us, "Everything hath He made beautiful in its proper time . . ."

Jo continued to study art at the Alliance. He knew many of the models well. Some were his neighbors. Some owned pushcarts, which he passed daily. Several were friends of his family and members of the same synagogue.

There was old Reuben Mendyl, who sold children's socks and underwear. Here at the Alliance, old Reuben, sitting so stiffly, was not the old Reuben Jo waved to each morning. That old Reuben always had a carefree smile and a funny phrase to banter. Jo knew why old Reuben sat here now. An underwear pushcart is hard work, especially in winter. People stopped at the food pushcarts, but they might not bother with the underwear pushcart until the day was sunny and warm. So for fifteen cents an hour old Reuben had consented to come to the Alliance and pose for the art students. But he was not happy about it! He was unused to being indoors. Unused to sitting in one position. Not used to being the object of all eyes. He disliked having people look at him as if he was not a real live person, but only an object intended to be drawn on a sheet of paper. Jo watched him carefully and saw unwept tears in old Reuben's eyes. The strong hands which pushed the heavy cart tried to stay still, but they trembled. The shoulders hunched. No, this was not Jo's old Reuben. Jo's old Reuben was altogether special. Where was *that* old Reuben now?

"I've a pair of your socks on, Reuben! My sister, Rose, bought them. Three pairs you sold her only last week. Eighteen cents and already the second time I wear them, there's a hole!"

Old Reuben's eyes brightened. His sense of salesmanship began to stir.

"What are you saying?" he demanded, lifting his head and meeting Jo's eyes. "That by me the merchandise is not the best?" His voice became stronger. "Well let me tell you, Jo Davidson, and everyone else who is listening. Reuben Mendyl's socks is the finest yet! By me is only high class stock. If holes is coming is because your feet is making them!"

"Oh come now, Reuben!" Jo said, beginning to make quick, sure lines on his paper. "Are you saying my feet are too big?"

"Reuben Mendyl is not saying by you or anybody the feet is too big. Reuben Mendyl is saying only by him everything is strictly first class. Underwear and socks all top grade! Nobody gets stuck buying from Reuben Mendyl's pushcart. And that's the truth. Better yet I should starve!"

By this time, old Reuben's head was held high, the weary old eyes shone with pride, the strong hands were firm and steady. Old Reuben was talking about something he knew and because it was so, he relaxed completely. Jo's chatter had made him act himself! Now the students drew enthusiastically. Here was a real model! The high cheeks, the rich curved mouth. That Jo Davidson could talk a model into anything. Why this one was worth at least *twenty* cents an hour!

Or perhaps the dignified cantor of the Ezrath Israel synagogue was posing. He was a calm one, this Rabbi Moishe Rabinowitz. He looked at no one. He just sat. To draw him was to draw a rock with the faint lines the weather had made in it, but always the rock was cold, hard, and set. No, Rabbi Moishe Rabinowitz was not a good model. Besides, how did you get him to relax? He was a dignified, learned man. He talked only to scholars. You couldn't have him sing, for he would not sing his holy songs outside the synagogue or away from the Sabbath table. Oh, there was no question about it—this was a difficult model to draw. Jo frowned in thought. There had to be something to make Rabbi Rabinowitz act naturally.

"Rabbi?"

"Yes," the man answered.

"My mother tells me you have the voice of an angel! You made her weep last Shabbos."

"Thank you." The voice remained polite, but it was cold as the man was cold. Jo bit his lip, thought harder. He had not put down so much as a single line on his paper and class was almost over! He simply couldn't let this happen.

"Rabbi," he asked cheerfully, not feeling cheerful at all, "When you were a boy my age, could you sing any other songs than holy ones?"

Rabbi Rabinowitz' brow crinkled a little. "So what kind of songs would I sing?"

"I was just thinking you couldn't always have sung just in the synagogue, although my mother says no one in all New York knows so many Hebrew songs as you."

"That may be so." The rabbi's voice quavered a bit as he demanded, "And who is there who can learn enough songs in Jehovah's name?"

"It is wonderful, Rabbi, but are there other songs—any songs at all—that you can sing besides synagogue ones? Why, I'll bet I know songs you've never even heard of!"

"Is that so? Well, you'd be surprised!" The rabbi snapped his fingers and suddenly a small twinkle crept into his clear blue eyes.

"What for instance?" asked Jo.

"Well, long ago—eight years it was, I first come to New York and what do I know? Some Russian, Yiddish of course, and Hebrew. English I have only a little. But I listen and I learn! My friend, Officer Flanagan—over on Rivington Street—helped me. He taught me 'Believe Me If All Those Endearing Young Charms.' Also, I learn 'Oh Susanna' and 'Dixie.' " The rabbi's foot began to beat a little rhythm and his lips hummed a melody.

"You still know all the words to 'Dixie'?" Jo asked. "Why, I learned that one in school myself, but I never thought anyone like you would know it too!"

"What a *chutzpa ponem* you are!" Rabbi Rabinowitz shook his head. "Such a lot you have to learn, so just listen!"

With that, the rabbi sang "Dixie," "Oh Susanna," and all the other songs he could think of, and his foot beat time and he had all he could do to keep his beautiful long hands from clapping. His drab white beard turned to silver fire and his large eyes softened with pleasure.

The class began to draw as it never had before. Models were always so good when that Jo Davidson was around! So full of life. If only they always had such models. And Jo, smiling to himself, thought about how magical words can be and made the best sketch of all!

3. Medicine or Art?

At sixteen, Jo still attended classes at an evening high school, where he learned to make drawings from plaster casts. On Saturdays and Sundays, Jo and his friend, Sam Halpert, walked blocks and blocks from East Side New York to the vast halls of the Metropolitan Museum of Art on upper Fifth Avenue.

"Here come those same two kids again," one guard would remark to another. "If one of them doesn't turn out to be a famous artist someday, it will only be because somebody tied his hands behind his back permanently."

"It's going to take more than that to stop that kid with the black wavy hair," the other guard said then. "Ever notice how his eyes light up when he sees something he likes? Tie his hands behind his back and he'll learn to paint with the brush in his mouth!"

It was almost that bad for Jo. Every spare moment he had—and he had all too few—he would either sketch or try to learn something about the technique of drawing. If only there was money enough to go to a regular school to study art! But there wasn't. All the money Jo earned, he gave his mother to help out at home and tried to content himself with the Alliance classes or the brief moments in evening school.

Jo's eldest sister, Nancy, had married a young doctor, David Bercinsky, and now lived in New Haven, Connecticut. David was having a hard time getting started in his practice, and although he wanted to help Jo, he could do no more at the time than offer him a room in his house.

Only Rachie understood how much Jo wanted to get ahead. By now, she was teaching and she told everyone whom she met about her brother. She carried sketches along with her just to show what he had done. "Now you just look at this! See how clever he is with people? Notice this woman's smile! You can see she's found a real bargain and is pleased as a kid with a red lollipop. And look how painstaking he's been about this man's mustache. Makes you almost yearn to get out the scissors and trim it, doesn't it? And he's never had any real training at all. I just know if he ever had a real chance, he'd be a famous artist!"

People looked at what Rachie had to show them and they saw what Rachie saw. Unlike Rachie, they didn't quite understand how important it all was. They agreed Jo was talented, but that was all. But Rachie was not discouraged. She went right on talking.

"I won't give up!" she said stubbornly. "Jo must have a chance to prove himself. He can draw—better than most people can even imagine and somewhere there has to be someone who will help him."

Then one fine day, someone did hear and understand what all of it meant. Rachie met an old friend, and as always, she took out Jo's sketches. The friend looked and saw the beginnings of great ability in Jo's rude sketches. That night Rachie danced on the sky!

"Oh Jo! It's all come true at last. He's going to pay your tuition for a whole year in the evening classes at the Art Students' League."

Jo was overwhelmed. His heart, that heart which

was to grow larger and more filled with understanding
all the days of his life, almost burst with the fierceness
of its beating. At long, long last, he was really on the
way. Now he had a chance to learn how to be a real
artist. Now he'd make the entire family proud of him.

You would have thought that everything was settled,
but it wasn't. At home, things were all mixed up again.
Nobody was pleased by the news about Jo except
Rachie. Everyone else, even his beloved mother, had
decided it was better for Jo to become a doctor.

Because the Davidsons were a close family, they
always talked over their problems together. They
talked now about what the medical profession had to
offer in comparison with art. It was not because Rachie
loved Jo more than the rest that she wanted to help
him become an artist. It was simply that she understood how important it was for him to do what he most
wanted to do himself. Nor was it that Jo's parents
loved him less that they wanted him to be a doctor.
They felt that no matter what one chooses to do in this
world, the struggle is never easy and they wanted their
son to select a career they believed would be more
secure and rewarding.

"A doctor means something in a community, Jo.
Maybe there isn't any reason for it, but people always
seem to think of an artist as an odd person—that is, if
they think about him at all!"

"But, Mother, I don't care what people think. I only care about doing what I believe is best for *me!*"

"No, Jo." Haya smiled one of her quick, sweet grins. "You do care. You must! Whatever you do, you will always care about people and what they think. And it's right that you should think so because we are forever part of the world we live in."

Jo was silent then. He knew his mother spoke the truth. He listened while she went on.

"Son, believe me, we don't mean to keep you back from what you want to do. Take your gift and try it. Then you'll see how right we are! When the year is up at art school, go to New Haven and stay with Nancy and David and you can study medicine at Yale. I'm sure you'll find what everyone else finds—that the things we think we want to do as children must be put aside. It's part of growing up!"

"But what if Jo still wants to be an artist at the end of the year?" Rachie insisted, "What then?"

"Oh, but that won't happen!" Jo's father sounded certain. "This is only a passing idea Jo has. Wait until he studies medicine! He'll enjoy it so much he'll wonder whatever made him think about art."

Jo sat still. He wished that he could agree with his parents. But he felt they were wrong. Maybe medicine was exciting—but was it for *him?* He liked Nancy's husband, David. He was a wonderful person, but perhaps that was because medicine seemed so right for him. It was certainly the one thing David wanted to do above all else. And yet—if David liked it so much, then there must be something to it.

"All right, I'll go to Yale," Jo said at last, wondering why he felt so sad. "But first, I'm going to take everything I can for a year at the Art Students' League."

Rachie patted his shoulder and ran out of the room. Rose, who had stood by silently throughout the discussion, leaned over and swiftly kissed him. His mother took his hand.

"Don't worry, Jo. Everything will be fine."

Jo nodded, not quite so sure.

His father smiled radiantly.

Once again, Jo worked during the day and studied at night. There was so much to learn at the Art Students' League and he had so little time for learning it. While he studied, he remembered one of the most fascinating Bible stories he knew, always a favorite of his. The story of David and Goliath. Jo saw David so clearly in his mind that he knew exactly how David looked at the exact moment he raised his sling. He made a sketch of David and entered it in a contest he had read about.

He met another young student at the League. His

name was Waterbury and he was fortunate enough to have his own studio. Waterbury showed Jo how to paint on a piece of leather, on which an outline of a drawing had been burned with a needle. This was called pyrography and it was quite fashionable in our grandparents' time.

Jo went out and got a job doing this sort of work during the day. Later on, he did the same sort of thing using wood instead of leather.

On Saturdays and Sundays now, he attended the Country Sketch Club, where he once again worked from models.

One Sunday, a rather interesting discussion came up and Jo was worried about it, for it suddenly seemed as if there was something missing in his way of painting—in the art he loved so well to do.

He had worked rather rapidly on the day's model—a lovely young woman with hair the color of his mother's wedding ring and eyes the green of a new spring leaf. On Jo's drawing, her hair was pale and her eyes seemed vague. As always, he had caught her facial expression exactly!

"Jo," the instructor looked at his drawing carefully, "No one here has gotten the set of head as well as you, and I, for one, only wish I could get as much action into a hand as you can. But your colors, boy—what in heaven's name has happened to them?"

"Gosh, I thought I had them! I see them plainly enough on the model, but when I put them on paper, something seems to happen to them."

"Close your eyes, Jo. Can you see red sharply with your eyes closed?"

Jo tried it, then shook his head. He could see red, but not clearly!

"Blue? Or orange?"

"It's no good! I can't. I can see colors clearly when I look at them, but if I turn my head away, I can't seem to see them mentally."

The teacher lowered his head and suddenly became interested in a button on his jacket. The two students nearest Jo began to paint furiously, although they had only played at their work before.

They don't have to spare my feelings, Jo thought, and they don't have to say it either. I *know*. I haven't as sharp a color sense as a good painter should have!

He went home, locked himself in his room, and concentrated with all his might for hours. Tried thinking about purple, about yellow. Of nothing but red. Red, red, *red!* But hard as he thought, he could not see them sharply in his mind. At last he knew that no matter how hard he tried, no mater how much he wanted, without an absolute color sense, he could never become a really great painter.

Perhaps, after all, it was just as well that his parents had made up their minds that he was to be a doctor!

Jo was deeply grieved when his art lessons came to an end. He was eighteen now and knew he must begin to study in order to pass the examinations for Yale Medical School. He had had little formal education and no college work at all, so it was going to be quite a task. He would have to spend almost every hour of the summer at it, if he was to pass at all. How could he possibly do it?

He went to Connecticut to stay with Nancy and David while he studied. He saw at once that things were extremely difficult for David, who was only beginning his practice, and once again Jo felt he had to help out. Yet how was it possible when he had so much studying to do? At night, he tossed restlessly, fretting about it. There had to be a way. And then he had an idea!

He went to see the college photographer, Mr. Randall.

"I wonder if you would be good enough to lend me some photographs of Doctor Hadley, the President of Yale?" Jo wanted to know and went on to explain. "I'm rather good at doing burnt wood panels, and I'd like to do one of him, if I may."

Mr. Randall looked at Jo carefully. After all, he could take all the photographs of Dr. Arthur Hadley that anyone could wish, and granted photography was still fairly new, he was an expert who turned out a fine job. Why help someone else—someone he didn't even know—do a different type of portrait? Why, it would be just one less photograph he would be able to make and sell himself. And yet, there was something about this young man; the air of sincerity, the pleasant manner, the warm smile. . . . Mr. Randall decided to help him.

Between studying for examinations, Jo completed a portrait of Doctor Hadley on a three-ply wood panel. Then he took it back to show to Mr. Randall, who looked at it and decided to display it in his shop window.

Jo was elated. Perhaps if someone saw the panel, they might offer him a job doing leather pillows or burnt wood decorations. He could figure out a way later to do the job, study, pass his examinations, and still go to medical school. If only someone liked that wood panel—then there would be a job and he could really help Nancy and David!

Next day, Jo walked over to Mr. Randall's shop again. He wanted to see again how his panel looked in the window, but the window was surrounded with people! He joined them, as if he too was a passer-by, and almost gasped with astonishment when he saw that his wood panel of Doctor Hadley was marked "SOLD." He rushed into the store then, and learned from Mr. Randall that it had been bought by an attorney, Mr. William S. Pardee. More than that, Mr. Pardee wanted to meet the artist!

Mr. Pardee took Jo to lunch and introduced him to Professor Neimeyer of the Yale Art School. He had told Jo to bring along some of his sketches and when Professor Neimeyer looked at them, he invited Jo to attend Yale Art School at once.

"There isn't anything in the world I'd rather do!" Jo said, "but I'm studying medicine right now." He turned his head aside and pretended to look for something so that he wouldn't have to look at the professor and Mr. Pardee while he told them the rest. "I—I really don't have enough funds for what I'm supposed to do. That's why I made the panel of Doctor Hadley in the first place. I thought if it was good enough, perhaps someone would offer me a job and then I'd have money enough to . . . to. . . ." But it was useless. He couldn't finish what he had to say. He wasn't ashamed of his poverty. He had never been ashamed of *that*. But always, even as a young boy, he had been ashamed to complain, no matter how bad things were.

"I understand, Jo," the professor said, "but I'm afraid it's you who does not understand. You see, we need young men with real talent. Our art classes here are filled with boys who 'take' classes only because they have to, and they're not the least bit interested. Perhaps you don't even have enough money to buy a newspaper, but my art classes are open to you whenever you want to come!"

Slowly—not quite believing, Jo turned his head back to face these newfound friends. He could only nod his head, too filled with joy to express the gratitude he felt. Now he could continue to study medicine as he had promised to do, and there would be free art lessons besides!

Jo passed examinations for medical school and found his work there only beginning. He never dreamed there was so much homework in the world! Right now, this Saturday afternoon, he should have been in his room studying. Instead, here he was touring the Art School Building. He strolled into each class room, examined the drawings which hung on the walls, uncovered some of the sketches which stood about on easels. He picked up pastel crayons and charcoals, fingered paper, smelled paint. No, he decided, there isn't anything like it. Art is the one thing in the world—no, the universe, for me! But even as he thought about it, his conscience reminded him he was to be a doctor.

He went downstairs to the first floor of the Art

School and right at the front door—the one he should
have opened to go outside and back to his room to
study—the basement stairs caught his eyes. *What was
downstairs in the basement of an Art School?* Were
there drawings there such as the ones in the classrooms?
Or simply stacks of supplies? He snapped his fingers at
the front door!

"I'll be back and out in a jiffy!" he told the door,
"but first I must go downstairs and explore."

So off he went, down the steps. What an immense
place it was! Part of it was divided into shelving to hold
art supplies. He'd never seen so many brushes, so much
chalk and charcoal in his life! Where should he begin?
But of course there was only one place to begin—at the
beginning. He would start from the bottom of the
steps where he stood and walk up and down each inch
of basement until each sheet of paper was personally
known to him. And so, Jo Davidson explored. He
walked for hours, seeing, touching, smelling. He began
—although he didn't understand it at all—to have a
sense of inner excitement. His heart beat faster. His
footsteps echoed so loudly Jo was certain the dean
himself must hear them in his house. He stopped again,
looking all around. He'd seen almost everything there
was to be seen. All the fresh supplies, some old drawings previous students had made, pastels, easels, molds.
There was nothing left to look at but some aged, un-

attractive barrels in a far corner of the room. Yet there was this strange feeling he had. He had never had anything like it before. It was almost as if he was about to be born! He shook his head in confusion and once more looked all about him. No, there was nothing. He'd seen everything there was to see—except those old barrels. His heart, which had beat so fast it almost fluttered, seemed to have stopped completely now. Something wonderful had been about to happen—and now it was gone! He wrinkled his nose. There was a strange, oddly perfumed odor coming from the old barrels. An odor which made him think of the smell of earth when he had lain on it and buried his head in the grass. A clean, warm smell. It filled his lungs and head. He felt almost giddy. Suddenly he ran to the nearest barrel, reached in and let his fingers dig into its contents. He pulled out his hand and looked at the gray-green wad of clay in it! It felt cool in his palm. Cool and solid. Like the earth! He rolled it round. He pressed his fingers in it and his fingers left marks. He twisted it and it stayed twisted! He rolled it back again, poked three small holes in it, making a mouth and two eyes, and he had a comic face in clay. By now, his heart beat so fiercely again that his ears resounded with it. This—why, this was more than fun! With this clay, he could shape anybody or anything in the world and it would stay that way. No matter what anyone else in the whole world wanted of him, only this small lump of clay answered his own need!

After a while, Jo raised his head, looked about him, still holding the mass of clay in his hand. He noticed a plaster cast of St. Francis nearby and decided to try to copy it.

It never occurred to him that he might not be able to do it! He simply went right ahead as easily as he had let his hands dig into the barrel and began to make his own St. Francis. Only when he had nearly finished did he realize that someone was watching him!

He whirled around to see that it was Mr. Boardman, one of the art instructors.

Oh, Jo thought, suddenly realizing what he had done, what will he do to me? Will I be expelled? But Mr. Boardman looked past Jo and studied the mask. It's all over now, Jo decided. Probably the worst mess Mr. Boardman has ever seen! And I've helped myself to the school's supplies without even asking. Besides, I have no business being here this time of the week.

"Davidson!"

"Yes—yes sir!"

"How long have you been working in clay?"

"I never did any before, sir. I mean—this is the first time. I wanted to see what was in the basement of the Art School and. . . . I am sorry, sir. Very sorry."

"What?" Mr. Boardman looked directly at Jo for

the first time. "Are you standing there telling me this is your *first* piece—your very first piece in clay?"

Jo nodded.

"That's incredible, boy! Unbelievable! Do you realize what you've done?"

Jo was confused now. It would serve me good and right, he thought, if Mr. Boardman throws me out this minute. I wonder how much clay is worth? Maybe I could pay him back for what I've wasted. I haven't got much with me—I think about eighteen cents maybe, but if I offer to make up for what I've used, maybe he'll overlook things!

"Davidson!" Mr. Boardman grabbed his shoulders. "Am I correct that you're a medical student?"

"Yes sir."

"Well, get out immediately!" Mr. Boardman almost shouted. "You're no doctor. You're a sculptor. A born sculptor! If this is your first piece, Heaven only knows what you can do with some training!"

Jo's mouth fell open. What Mr. Boardman was saying was the last thing he had expected to hear.

"Do you really mean it?"

"You bet I do, boy! This is the real thing. Don't let it get away. Go after it. You weren't meant to do anything else!"

Jo held out his hand timidly, his strong fingers still

covered with the clay, and Mr. Boardman gripped it, held it tightly, and smiled reassuringly.

Jo sighed then, a huge sigh filled with all the hopes of his young life. His feeling about the clay hadn't been wrong. As long as he lived, he never wanted to be or do anything else. God willing, he never would!

4. Learning—the Hard Way!

What a busy year it had been! Here it was 1903 and Jo was twenty! Americans were all set for a great fair at St. Louis. Had there ever been such an exciting time in history? Of course, the newspapers carried other items besides the fair. There was something about two brothers, Orville and Wilbur Wright, who flew a con-

traption they'd invented. It was called an "aeroplane."
And there was a new play by that strange Irishman,
George Bernard Shaw. The papers also carried news
about Helen Keller too, a remarkable young girl from
the South, who was blind and deaf. She was soon to
graduate from Radcliffe College, where she had taken
all the regular courses with the rest of the students!
Yes, Jo thought, the world's so full of outstanding
people, all of them making history. If only I could
have a small part of it!

He had left Yale Medical School at vacation time
and returned to New York. His parents hadn't been
happy about it, although his mother had tried hard to
understand.

"I know I may fail at what I want to do, Mother.
And yet, I simply have to try."

"All right, Jo," she agreed. "Take a chance. If you
fail, you're still my son. If you succeed, you're '*my*
sculptor.'"

She's such a swell sport, Jo thought. I've failed her
already, but someday I'll make it up to her. Someday,
she'll know I made the right choice.

He knew his father was bitterly disappointed. Jo
tried to tell him how he had felt about handling the
clay, but he saw it was no use. Jacob Davidson had his
own ideas about what he wanted for his son. The life
of an artist was not one of them.

Jo went back to the Art Students' League and learned that Herman A. MacNeil was teaching the sculpture groups. He asked Mr. MacNeil if he could work with him. Mr. Boardman's encouraging words were still fresh in his mind and Jo felt certain sculpturing was the one right thing in the world for him.

"Done any sculpturing?" Mr. MacNeil asked.

"Oh yes," Jo said, trying to be casual and thinking about Mr. Boardman's enthusiasm. "At Yale Art School."

Mr. MacNeil asked a few more questions, then decided to see what Jo could do on his own. He left Jo with a blueprint and a project to work on while he went on an errand. It was the first blueprint Jo had ever seen! For a moment, he nearly gave in and wondered if his father shouldn't have forced him to return to medical school at once. Then, as quickly, he made up his mind to have a try at Mr. MacNeil's project.

By the time Mr. MacNeil returned, Jo had made a little progress—enough so that Mr. MacNeil offered him a job as a studio boy in his Long Island place. And there it was that Jo first learned that his learning had only begun. At home, he talked of nothing else. As usual, Rachie was the only one who really listened to him and wanted to know even more.

"You know, Rachie, sculpture isn't like anything else

in art. I stand on one side of a form and I have to imagine how it will look from the other side. I never had to worry how the back of a sketch would look because there wasn't any."

"I never thought about it that way, Jo, yet I see what you mean. A statue is something a person can walk all around and it must be right, no matter where he stands. No wonder it's so difficult to do!"

Jo worked for Mr. MacNeil for four dollars a week. Most of what he made went for carfare, for it was quite a distance between the East Side of New York and Mr. MacNeil's Long Island studio. But Jo knew, as he had always known, that he mustn't stop, even though money was badly needed at home. Once again, he would have to continue with his job and find a way to help his family.

One day, Mr. MacNeil's gardener didn't show up for work and Jo asked for his job. He got it, which meant he slept at the studio, rose at sunup, worked in the garden until eight, worked in the studio until five, then back in the garden until sunset. All this for ten dollars a week! Once, he was the model for the legs of one of the statues Mr. MacNeil was making for the St. Louis Fair. Oh yes, Jo was going to be a sculptor all right and he was going to learn everything there was to learn. Only why did it always have to be the hard way?

When Mr. MacNeil's work for the St. Louis Fair was completed, he had to let Jo go. He gave him a letter to the man in charge of sculpture at the fair, since sculptors were still needed on the grounds. Jo was eager to go, but as usual he was out of money. He had sent home almost every penny of the ten dollars a week he had earned.

Once more, he had to find a means, so he worked his way out to St. Louis selling wafers of the sort used for ice cream sandwiches. By the time he arrived in St. Louis, no more sculptors were needed and Jo was alone in a strange city, homeless and jobless. Because it was fair time, the city was filled and even the smallest room was terribly expensive. Jo took what was probably "the smallest room," but even so it took almost all the money he had earned to pay for it.

He wandered around the fair, looking for a job, and finally found one at his old craft—pyrography. This time he did profiles on leather cushions. He did one of Geronimo, the last of the great Indian chiefs. Geronimo, who had been visiting the fair, liked what Jo had done and was so well pleased that he came to the boarding house where Jo was staying and posed for him there.

When the fair was over, Jo worked his way East to Atlantic City, where he became "a sand artist." He piled sand into forms, making it into the faces of Indian chiefs or dancers, swimmers, acrobats and such. In between, he drew profiles of the people who leaned over the boardwalk rails to watch him. He worked hard, but he made very little, and even then he was so honest that he wouldn't charge for the profiles he drew unless the person drawn really liked the job!

During these years, Jo had many adventures, some embarrassing, some amusing, some unhappy—all of them the sort of thing that can happen to a young man away from home, trying to make his way in an unfamiliar world. But no matter how badly things went, Jo never gave up thinking about being a sculptor and having shows of his own. More and more, he thought about the sketch he had once made of David and Goliath. He had sent the sketch away and it had won an "Honorable Mention" in a competition. What would the sketch be like if he had made it into a piece of sculpture instead? If only he could get back to New York! Perhaps then, he could get to see Mr. Pardee, the man who had bought the burnt wood panel of Dr. Hadley. Perhaps Mr. Pardee, a short ride away from New York, might again be willing to help him. Or would he?

On a five dollar loan from a friend, Jo went home. He had only one thought in mind—to get started on a sculptured figure of David. He felt certain he understood what had gone on inside the David of the Bible thousands of years ago. Across the centuries, the mind of that other young boy seemed to reach out to him and say, "I conquered *my* giant, Jo. Can you conquer yours?"

Jo went to see Mr. Pardee in Connecticut, holding close to him the sketch of the David he wanted to sculpture. Indeed, one might have thought the figure would run off the paper and escape. If only Mr. Pardee likes it, Jo thought, why then it will be more than a sketch. I'll do it in bronze and people cannot only look at it—they'll be able to *feel* it as well. It will have form, as the human body has form, with a profile, a front and a back. A back! What sketch or painting has so much? No wonder Jo was nervous as he held out the sketch so Mr. Pardee could examine it. What if Mr. Pardee turned him down? But Mr. Pardee looked at the sketch briefly, then turned to Jo and smiled.

"I think this is grand, Jo. It should make an excellent piece of sculpture. Go on and make it up in bronze for me."

Back home in New York, the Art Students' League gave Jo a room to work in in exchange for having Jo teach summer class. His cousin, Itzel, consented to be the model for David.

Now at last, Jo decided, I'm really on my way. My

dream has come true. Maybe it had—in many ways. Certainly, there was money enough from Mr. Pardee for materials and the idea of doing David in bronze was a good one. More than that, Jo had a place to work and an excellent model. And he was near his beloved family too. There was just one thing wrong—he just couldn't seem to settle down to work! The dream was complete in every way except the *doing*, and the *doing*, of course, was the most important thing of all.

Jo drew Itzel in a dozen poses, none of them much better than what he had drawn originally. He doodled and he dawdled. But he accomplished nothing. Now he began to wonder if he would ever really be a sculptor. Did he really know how to "buckle down"? One day his friend and fellow artist, Edward McCarten, stopped by and watched Jo trying to work. He watched Jo as long as he could stand it, shook his head, and then gave Jo a piece of advice that was never to be forgotten.

"When you get here tomorrow, Jo, go to work as if this is your last day on earth and you have to finish your statue before you die!"

Jo stared at McCarten in astonishment, then nodded in understanding. Of course, that was the only way to do it. After all, had David stood around waiting for Goliath to decide things? It might have been David's last day on earth too, but he hadn't let a second of it go to waste. Slingshots needed not only courage and faith—they also needed a fast draw. . . .

Jo really went ahead now and the two-foot statue was rapidly completed. Mr. Pardee came to New York and liked it so well, he ordered an extra copy. Next, the Society of American Artists accepted it to show in their annual exhibition, giving Jo the first official recognition he had had as an artist.

Jo, in a borrowed suit, and Rachie, dressed as well as she could manage on her slim salary, attended the show. Both of them were so excited they weren't actually sure it was happening, even though they were both there to see it. Was it really so? But it must be because there was Jo's "David" right in the middle of the portraits, landscapes, and sculptures by artists famous the world over. Besides, you could touch "David" and he felt exactly the way Jo had always imagined. His statue had a profile, a front, and best of all a back.

Now Jo began to spend almost all his time at the Art Students' League. He made other busts, including one of his mother, showing clearly the worn face, with the serene brow and the mouth always so ready for stories and laughter.

"If I just breathe on it," Rachie said, surveying it from all sides, "just the lightest whisper, Jo, I'm sure it will come alive and be more than a bust. Then we'll have two mothers! And how can there possibly be two mothers as wonderful as ours?"

Yes, it was a fine job Jo had done and one of which he could truly be proud, but somehow it failed to be accepted the way "David" had been.

"Don't worry, Jo," his mother comforted him. "Someday, you'll be famous, and then I'll say you've been *my* sculptor from the beginning!"

"You mustn't mind, Jo," Rachie consoled. "What matters is that *you* know this bust is good. Someday, others will know it too."

Jo didn't say much about the bust. He knew Rachie was right, for he had put into the bust of his mother all he knew she was and someday other people would understand and see it too. He had already learned in part how to steel himself against the times he would fail. There were always such times—for everyone. Had it not taken Moses forty years to lead the people out of the wilderness? How many times during those long years had it seemed easier to go back to Egypt? Yes, Jo came of a people who could wait out the setbacks of life.

As always at the Art Students' League, there were many talented boys and girls. Some were Jo's friends and advisers. One in particular became a special companion. Her name was Florence Lucius. She was a tall, dark girl, swift in movement, gracious in manner. Her eyes were a near-purple color, full of merriment, and her skin was a soft glow. She was not pretty in the usual sense, yet when she spoke and moved, she made everyone else in the room seem plain! Florence was a sculptor too and perhaps better than anyone else, even Rachie, understood what Jo was trying to do, because she knew from personal experience how much craftsmanship went into the work. She was fond of music, books, and sports, and it seemed to her as if there wasn't enough time in the world for her to do and learn all the things she was interested in. Life was so exciting, so full of fun! Jo became a regular visitor at her home, where he would announce himself at the front door by playing a little tune on the bell. Da-da-da-da-DUM-DUM!

"That's Jo," Florence would say, running to answer the door. "He even has fun with doorbells."

Florence's father, a prominent civil engineer, thought there was nothing quite so important and right as science, but he delighted in Jo's company. Jo was so different from most people he generally met. Mr. Lucius would rub his hands together gleefully at the sound of that doorbell, knowing it meant an interesting time for him too.

"Fine. That's fine. Jo Davidson—there's nobody in the world I enjoy so much in an argument!"

Then Jo would enter the room and there the three

of them would sit, talking into the early morning hours. The talk was lively, amusing, and instructive. Each of them learned from it.

Whenever Florence visited Jo's home, she never ceased to be astonished that his mother and sisters greeted him as if they hadn't seen him for weeks. He was that kind of person—always so exciting. He brought life into the room with him. Perhaps it was because he always seemed to mean what he said and his eyes sparkled so with understanding and humor. His enthusiasm was contagious.

Florence would play an air by Mozart on the piano —there was only one that she knew well, yet no matter how often she played it, everyone thought it charming. After all, wasn't she playing it to make them happy?

Then there was the phonograph to listen to, the big old-fashioned kind that RCA still uses for a trademark (with a small dog listening to "His Master's Voice" coming out of an enormous horn).

"It's Melba," Florence would say dreamily, seeing in her mind's eye the great star of the Metropolitan Opera. "Oh, wouldn't it be marvelous to have a voice like hers?"

"I like your voice, Flossie," Jo would say. "I think it's a lovely voice. Besides, it always says just the things I want to hear!"

And Florence would blush and think what a nice boy Jo was and how much fun it was to be with the Davidsons. Jo's mother would get out the huge samovar she'd brought with her from Russia, put it on a handsome brass tray, and serve tea.

"Such delicious strawberries," Flossie would say, asking for a second helping. "I've tried and tried to do them this way myself, but something always happens, and they never taste nearly so good."

Jo's mother would smile at Flossie and think what a sweet girl she was. How she hoped Jo saw it too.

It seemed to Flossie afterward—even long, long years afterward—that the talk, the music, the being together, was never as good as it had been then. There was something so different about those days. The Davidson family was so special. Or maybe it was Jo. He was extra special. But when she thought about him in particular, she found herself blushing and pushed the thought aside.

And Jo, who had always found it so easy to talk to everyone else somehow didn't manage to get around to telling this wonderful young girl, until years and years afterward, that he kept making the long trip all the way out to Brooklyn just to see her. . . .

5. Exodus!

Jo was in his twenties now, working industriously on small projects, teaching in exchange for the room in which he worked. Each day he became more concerned because he didn't seem to be making the progress he had hoped. Nothing seemed to go right for him these days.

The failure with his mother's bust upset him more than anyone knew. He had intended that bust to express motherhood everywhere. When he made it, he kept remembering an old Jewish proverb, "God could not be everywhere, so he made mothers." That was what the bust was meant to say to everyone who saw it, but how could anyone see it unless it was exhibited in an art show?

Outside Jo's small studio room, New Yorkers sang and hummed, "Give My Regards to Broadway," a new musical number. I'd like to "Give My Regards to Broadway," Jo thought. I'd like to get far enough away from it to do just that. He had forgotten how badly he had once wanted to come back to it. Only now, when he didn't seem to be making progress, all he cared to do was to go somewhere, do something— anything at all—which might take him further along the path he had chosen. Paris, for example. Paris was the one place in all the world to study art. Even the soil of France, rich in gypsum, was meant for a sculptor! No wonder so many artists went there to work.

People everywhere spoke about the artists and writers who were in Paris these days. There was the famous studio of Gertrude Stein and her brother, Leo. Gertrude and Leo had left America for Paris several years before and were already well known for fostering a new movement in art and writing as well. If they could do it, why couldn't he?

Jo knew he had much for which to be grateful, yet he was restless. How was he ever going to prove worthy of his family's love and trust? He must get going. If only he could get to Paris! Of course, he could ask Mr. Pardee. Certainly, there was no harm in trying. Mr. Pardee had already done so much for him. Would he understand this desire too? Well, there was nothing for it but to ask and find out, and so once again Jo went to Mr. Pardee. And once again, Mr. Pardee understood! That very week Jo bought a ticket for France.

Benjamin Franklin, that great American patriot, who in the later years of his life stayed in France as ambassador for the newly formed United States, once remarked, "*Chaque homme a deux patries, la sienne et la France.*" (Every man has two countries, France and his own.) For Jo, this was completely true. From the beginning, he loved France, accepting it as his home away from home.

Mr. Pardee had given Jo a hundred and fifty dollars for the trip. It had seemed like a fortune. Even when he found out that his ticket took most of this money, Jo wasn't upset. With Paris ahead, why worry over the price of a ticket? The finest teachers and the best schools and museums were in Paris. The richest soil. Artists of all kinds—poets, painters, composers—each of them thriving on one another's company. Who had time to worry about money?

When the boat docked, Jo's old friend, Edward McCarten met him.

"Jo, how grand to see you!"

"It's great to be here and having you meet me is more than I deserve."

"Wait until you hear the news, Jo! I've rented a studio for you to work in, and what's more, it's right next to my own."

Abruptly, Jo swallowed and found himself unable to answer. He was pleased, of course. McCarten was such a good friend, so thoughtful, so kind. But now Jo suddenly realized that the only money he had in the world was forty dollars. He wondered if he dared to ask what the studio would cost. He wondered what McCarten would say when he told him how much money he had—or rather *didn't* have. He wondered how he could tell this considerate friend what a chance he had taken in coming to a strange country where he didn't know the language and had scarcely any money on which to get along.

"What's wrong, Jo? You're not angry because I

went ahead and found a place for you? I assure you it has a fine light to work by. Excellent for a sculptor. And it's clean and warm and. . . ."

"It's not that," Jo sighed. "I'm not certain I'll be able to afford it."

"Oh, don't worry about money, Jo. It's not awfully expensive. Living in France is far cheaper than it is in the States. And with your lessons covered, the only real expense you'll have is the studio and food, and I promise you they are both reasonable."

"But my lessons aren't paid for."

McCarten stared at Jo, astounded. It wasn't possible. Everyone knew students who came to Paris to study usually came in one of two ways—either they had plenty of money to begin with, or they were on a scholarship so their lessons were paid for in advance. McCarten knew Jo was quite poor and couldn't possibly have enough money to pay his own way in class, so when Jo had written to tell him he was coming to Paris, McCarten instantly took it for granted that Jo had a scholarship. After all, anyone who had ever seen Jo's work knew how talented he was, and it was quite natural to think he had a scholarship. Now, McCarten shook his head numbly. For the life of him, he couldn't understand how Jo had dared take such a risk as this.

"But I simply had to come," Jo said, reading his friend's mind. "And there wasn't any other way. Or if there was, I'm afraid I didn't know it."

Finally, McCarten nodded. Of course, Jo *had* to come. It was the place he belonged. All the same, it was an awful chance to take.

"I suppose we'd better get started, Jo." McCarten bent down to pick up one of Jo's grips. "Though I swear it's completely beyond me how you're going to manage." He grinned a little. "Still, knowing you, you'll probably find a way."

Jo grinned back. Soon, both of them, arm in arm, made their way through the cobbled streets of Paris to Jo's first studio in France. And when at last he stood in it, bare as it was, small as it was, shabby, Jo thought it was the most splendid room he'd ever seen—even if he couldn't afford it!

Jo had to buy a few items of furniture for his studio, as well as some pots and pans, since he obviously was going to have to do his own cooking if he was to manage at all. By the time he had finished making these necessary purchases, there was little of his forty dollars left. He did have one important thing of his own, however—blankets and bedding. His mother had insisted on his taking them along.

"But nobody takes bedding to Paris, Mother. People will think I'm mad."

"So let them think. You take them. And wait and see—you're sure to need them too."

In vain, Jo had tried to escape taking these things along, but his mother was as stubborn in her way as he was in his. If Jo made sense, as he had about his name, she instantly gave in. When he had taken the wheels off his horse, she had accepted his reasoning. But this time, she felt she was right and she held firm to her beliefs. When they were arguing over the matter, Jo recalled how his father had read from the Bible that Jews are "a stiff-necked" people. Well, the Davidsons seemed to fit the description, and yet it was more than that, really. It was an absolute faith you either had or didn't.

And so Jo slept between his mother's bedding miles and miles away from his home, his parents, the ocean between them, and there were few nights indeed when he did not bless his mother for having been so "stiff-necked."

His friend, McCarten, had arranged for a milkman to leave Jo milk and butter, and for a baker to leave bread. Jo felt almost rich. He had enough to eat, enough to live on. After all, he had been hungry before and had always managed. Besides, he had a fine shelter and he would find a job. If only he could speak French! Why, he didn't know the word for the most important of all things—*clay*.

Later, McCarten took Jo to the American Art Association, a group that looked after American students and artists. Jo was given a job teaching English to a Frenchwoman. For Jo, the job was a complete success. Not only did he earn money, but *he* learned how to speak fluent French. Afterward though, he was never altogether sure if he had managed to teach the French lady how to speak English!

Now, I'm set, Jo thought. No matter what happens, I'm going to make good in Paris.

McCarten, unfailingly kind, took Jo around Paris to see the sights and introduce him to his friends, who often met at some of the small Parisian cafés. If Jo could manage, he sometimes spent an entire evening in places such as these, buying only a cup of coffee or a single glass of wine. His friend, Sam Halpert, who had shared so many Saturdays with him at the Metropolitan Museum in New York, had come to Paris to study too. But most often, Jo stayed by himself, working away in his room with whatever materials he had, trying to make something out of nothing.

"My mother used to do this with ground meat," he told himself one day. "Only she always seemed to succeed with it. I wonder if anyone has ever found ground clay good to eat!"

He never tried to find out what the clay tasted like, of course, although he was often tempted to do so, for he was genuinely hungry at times. Still, the thought that his mother had had to manage helped him immensely. He knew she must have often wondered how it would all end. Well, no matter—she had stuck and so would he!

One night, Jo made a few extra francs and arranged to meet a friend in one of the cafés where they could spend the night talking about art and all the things which were going on then. When they were about to leave the café, a Great Dane came into the place. The dog was obviously lost. Jo's friend tried to coax the animal to him, but the huge beast only bared his teeth and snarled. Jo stood quietly, observing. Then he reached into his as-usual empty pockets and felt about for change. He had only a few centimes left. He had had visions of an egg for breakfast or perhaps lunch next day. Or if not an egg, a small bit of meat. And if not an egg or a piece of meat, some clay. He was forever running out of clay. And yet. . . . He looked at the dog again and shook his head. He knew only too well what the animal's main problem was.

"André," he called to the waiter. "Please bring a bowl of bread and milk for the dog."

The waiter frowned. So did Jo's friend. Both of them knew how little money Jo had. Yet how could they refuse? There was authority in Jo's voice. He seemed to understand where they had not. Silently

André fetched the bread and milk and gave it to Jo, who put it down in front of the dog.

"Here friend, this is what you need."

When the beast finished, he raised his head, stared solemnly at Jo for a minute, then walked over to him. His great eyes acknowledged a new master. Jo called him "Sultan" because of his majestic bearing. And now he had an all-day companion to share his loneliness. Soon everyone in Paris knew the young artist and his dog and people often stopped to chat with them. Jo's enemy, loneliness, was at last defeated.

Jo had many discussions about art with a new friend, Louis de Kerstrat, a painter. One day they went together to see an exhibition at the Salon des Artists Independents (an independent art group). What a strange show it was, with all the displays in *tents!* The artists who exhibited here had tried to throw over all the old rules. They had begun to paint and sculpture in an altogether different manner than the way art was taught in the classroom. Some of the pieces were good, others awful. Some artists had tried to squeeze out the flavor from their subjects, the way one squeezes juice from an orange. The word for this sort of art is "Abstraction." Others felt it was an age of machinery, so they had painted machinery in their pictures. Some felt humor ought to be included, so they painted gay little figures and "squiggles." Others had used geometric forms, with mountains and trees in blocks—this is known as "Cubism." No matter what one thought of the work, beautiful or ugly, it was definitely new—and exciting! *Moving.* This was what Jo wanted to feel in his own work. Sometimes he felt stifled in the classroom.

For Jo, this new finding meant that he could work without "prettifying" people. Now he could do his models, not only as he saw them—without "straightening" a crooked nose or making "an even smile"—but he could express what he saw *within* them, as well as without.

Actually, although Jo did not realize it, what he had learned was not new at all, but an ancient lesson—this way of looking on the inside. For thus is it written in the Apocrypha, "For the Lord seeth not as a man seeth; for man looketh on the outward appearance, but the Lord looketh on the heart."

Jo was working hard these days and beginning to acquire a reputation as an excellent artist—and a fast one. In fact, he was so busy that when a friend asked him to go out on a double date with a girl, Yvonne, Jo wasn't interested enough to learn her last name.

Two months later, he met his old friend, Louis de

Kerstrat, now in military service, but home on leave. Louis asked Jo to meet his sister, Yvonne. It was the same girl Jo could have met two months sooner if he had not been so busy!

Jo hadn't forgotten Florence, but the letters they had exchanged so frequently when Jo first came to Paris had become fewer. Flossie too was busy with her own work and friends and they grew apart.

The artist in Jo responded instantly to Yvonne, for she was graceful and beautiful. His feeling for Yvonne was different than what he had known for Florence, for he was older now and the magic of what people always call "first love" was gone. Someday it would return, but Jo didn't know that then. And, after all, there are only a few people in all the world fortunate enough to find the magic of "first love" a *second* time!

On her part, Yvonne liked Jo's warmth and vitality. He was so much fun! She didn't even mind the heavy black beard he now wore. It seemed exactly right for him to have one. He looked like a dedicated young prophet.

When she met Jo, Yvonne had plans of her own, for she was a talented actress and was on her way to the United States to appear in a play. In vain, Jo pleaded with her to stay, but although he was working hard on the kind of busts he wanted to do, he still wasn't earn-ing very much and Yvonne had a promise of success on her own. How could he keep her back? And so she sailed, although both of them were sad at the idea of parting.

With more determination than ever, Jo plunged himself into his work. Sometimes he worked so rapidly that he was able to do a bust at a single sitting! It was remarkable too how alive they seemed—different from the usual stuffy forms people had become used to seeing. Before she left, Jo had made a bust of Yvonne. It was one of the few comforts he had, outside of her letters.

"Sultan," Jo would say, "why did we let her go away? We should have found a way to make her stay. We didn't work at it hard enough!"

And Sultan, his great head between his paws, as close to his master as he could get, seemed to understand. Even his tail wagged less these days.

Then one special day, the mail brought good news. Yvonne wrote she was giving up her career and coming back.

It would have been pleasant to write that Jo and Yvonne were married and lived happily ever afterwards, but this was life—a *real* life, and real life is never, even at best, easy.

By now Jo was doing far better, but he was still poor. Yvonne, like Jo's mother, was quite clever with her hands. She made and designed blouses, skirts, all sorts of things, trying to help out, but there wasn't enough money for them to get married and raise a family. Both of them worked as hard as they knew how, and yet somehow things seemed to go wrong. And then, as if things weren't hard enough, Yvonne fell ill! Now what do I do, Jo asked himself? I've got to find a way to take care of her. If only I could get together enough money! But try as he would, he made little headway.

He had a one-man exhibition in England and the critics gave it excellent reviews. The people who saw his work there liked it and said so plainly, but for all of that, only a single piece was sold.

His problem began to seem almost hopeless and he worried about it constantly. One day, he worried so much he neglected to feed Sultan. He sat by his studio window, head in hands, fretting, and unable to work. Finally, Sultan came over and tugged and tugged at his jacket until Jo looked up.

"Come with me, master," the dog seemed to plead, and Jo—sighing with despair, rose and followed the animal to the door, but when he opened the door, no one was there. No one and nothing—nothing, that is, but the bread which the baker had left early that morning and the milk, now warm, which Jo had also forgotten to take in. Sultan kept right on barking, first pulling at Jo's jacket, then nudging the container of milk, until at last his great tail knocked it over and now Jo had a mess to clean up. But just as he reached to mop it up, his eyes met the soft, intelligent eyes of his huge pet and he couldn't help but remember how it was when he first met. On that night too, there had been only bread and milk for Sultan!

"Like old times, isn't it, Sultan?" Jo smiled suddenly, and Sultan barked, almost as if he was saying a most emphatic "Yes!"

Jo watched the hungry beast gulp down the bread and milk, even as he had done that first night. Funny, Jo thought, how things happened that night—how they always seem to have a way of happening without our having too much to do with it. Somehow, something always comes along to help—just when a person thinks there's nothing left at all. Almost like the manna the Jews found in the desert thousands of years ago when they thought there was nothing left for them either! And remembering that, Jo suddenly had the answer he sought. Because he had not found the manna he needed, that didn't mean there wasn't any— maybe he had looked in the wrong places. Perhaps it was "back home," just waiting for him! After all, it had been "back home" that had made his "David" come true. Why hadn't he thought of it before?

Silently, he raised his eyes and looked out the large studio window into the starlit splendor of the night.

There are worlds out there, he thought, bigger than anything I can imagine. A universe greater than any man's ideas. And beyond and above it all, there is an *order* that never fails. A God so truly great He has time to lead a dog to a bowl of bread and milk. And furnish manna for the hungry!

Jo decided to take another chance and sail for home to see if he could secure a show of his pieces. If only there was enough money to take Yvonne with him, but as it was he had to borrow funds to pay his own passage.

Oddly enough, New York, that great city of progress, always first in so many things, had never had a one-man exhibition in sculpture. In one art gallery after another, Jo tried to obtain a show of his own. Everyone was courteous to him, but no one thought it was a good idea. Who had ever heard of an entire room full of sculpture all by the same man? What a strange idea!

All the comforting Jo received from his family didn't help. They understood his problem, but had no way of assisting him. As usual, Jo was stubborn. There had to be one place in New York where his works could be shown. Then one night Rachie had an idea.

"Do you remember, Jo," she asked thoughtfully, "that once you sold a sketch of a rabbi to a man by the name of George Hellman? Didn't Mr. Hellman have an art gallery?"

"Of course, I remember! He was as kind to me as he could be. Only I don't know where he is now and how could I possibly go up to him after all these years and say, 'Remember me? I'm the boy who sold you a sketch of Rabbi Rabinowitz'?"

"Perhaps one of your friends may know him, Jo. Then you wouldn't need to feel strange about asking. Besides, who knows? Mr. Hellman may remember that drawing. I don't think anyone who saw it would forget it."

As things turned out, a friend of Jo's did know George Hellman and offered to go along with Jo to inquire if Mr. Hellman would let him have a show at his gallery. But when they finally saw Mr. Hellman, it was only to be told that his gallery was about to be closed!

"But Mr. Hellman!" Jo argued eagerly, his dark eyes flashing, "wouldn't it be a wonderful thing to close up the gallery with the *first* one-man show of sculpture ever given in the United States? It would be a real 'send-off'!"

Mr. Hellman bit his lip in concentration. He had heard about Jo's work in recent years, but more than that he remembered the sketch of the rabbi he had bought long ago. It had been the face of a poet of

God and the young boy who had drawn it seemed to have caught the model's innermost thoughts. Quickly, George Hellman made up his mind. Why not? Why not a one-man sculpture show? He'd seen Jo's work when he was only beginning and if he had improved but slightly since then, it would be well worth doing.

"I'll do it, Jo. It may be a risk, but I'll do it anyway. It will be as fine a parting gesture as an art gallery ever had!"

Now that the show had been decided on, the work had just begun. Busts and statues had to be crated and shipped, uncrated and put on display. The simple business of having light "hit" a bust in the proper way could be a problem. It was rather like needing an electric lamp at the only part of the room where there is never an outlet!

From Paris, Yvonne wrote an unhappy letter. Louis, her brother and Jo's close friend, who had been happily married, had lost his wife suddenly. When Jo read the sad news, he was terribly upset. He realized at once what the loss meant to Louis and how he would feel if anything happened to Yvonne. He decided instantly that they must be married, money or no money! Success could wait. The important thing was to be together. He returned to Europe immediately, married Yvonne at once, and after the wedding he supervised the packing of his own pieces so they would arrive safely in New York. Then once again he had to leave Yvonne—there was still no money to take her along! Waving good-by from the boat, he wondered if he would ever have enough money. He didn't expect to make much as an artist—but if there was only enough so he could be with Yvonne and stay with her. The exhibition must succeed!

6. Covenant

The exhibit space Mr. Hellman gave Jo was in the basement of the gallery, but hundreds of people came to see it. A pamphlet listed all the pieces shown, and also contained some of Jo's own ideas about art and his work. Some of the statements were unquestionably sound, as when he wrote:

"A work of art is the expression of an emotion!"
Other things he said seemed a little foolish, perhaps, but Jo was still a young man and even the wisest of men does not acquire great wisdom for many years. Later on, Jo read some of the things he had written in that pamphlet and thought them a little absurd too. He always had an ability to laugh at himself—in fact, it was one of his nicest traits. Jo's personality helped in large measure to make his show a huge success. Newspaper and magazine critics were outspoken in their praise, not only of the work shown, but of Jo himself. One reporter in particular wrote that Jo's sculpture "had none of the dullness" which is so often found in work of this kind.

Mr. Hellman sold quite a few pieces and secured an order, or commission, for Jo to do a bust of Doctor Arthur Jacoby, the German Jew who had become one of America's most honored doctors. Jo made this bust for Mount Sinai Hospital in New York. Still another bronze was purchased by Mitchell Kennerley, the publisher, and Jo also made a bust of Mr. Hellman. He was extremely busy with his assignments and much better off financially than he had ever been, yet it still wasn't enough for his needs. He longed to return to France, but despite the success of his exhibition, it had not brought him enough to carry through his plans. His family was proud of him, and Jo kept

his unhappiness to himself, except for the moments
when he and Sultan, whom he had been able to bring
along, were alone.

"We haven't really done too badly, old fellow,"
he said, patting Sultan's long head, "But we're still
short."

Sultan, his graceful body for once sleek and well-
fed with the added comforts Jo was now able to give
him, nuzzled closer, trying to comfort his master.

"I wish you could talk, Sultan! Maybe you could
solve my problems for me sometime. I certainly don't
seem to be able to figure things out for myself right
now!"

But of course Sultan had no words and right now
that was what Jo needed—someone with whom he
could talk about what he wanted to do and how he
could set about doing it.

Then one night he had dinner with Mr. Kennerley
and several friends. After the others had left, Mr.
Kennerley urged Jo to tell him of what he planned in
the future. Jo was strangely silent. Mr. Kennerley was
surprised. He had never before seen this delightful
young man at a loss for words. In fact, he had found
Jo a most interesting companion because of his conversation.

"Is something the matter, Jo? I don't mean to pry,
but you actually look unhappy. Can I help?"

"No," Jo's voice was low. "There isn't anything anyone can do, really. It's a problem I've got to solve myself, I guess."

"We can talk about it at least. Sometimes just talking things over with a friend makes things easier."

Jo smiled. There was no reason why he shouldn't talk things over with Mr. Kennerley. True, always before he had thought other people's problems more important than his own. He always had the feeling he was strong enough to find a way and perhaps other people weren't. After all, God had given him a definite talent and other people had to go on, day in, day out, with no special gift at all. Still, what harm could it do now to discuss the situation?

"My problem isn't anything unusual, Mr. Kennerley. If I have money enough for materials for my work and for a model too, then I haven't enough to take care of my wife properly. I have enough money to go back to France without having to borrow for a change, but when I get there, I wouldn't have enough to look after Yvonne and go to work on a large project I've had in mind for months. I can do one thing or the other, but not both. And yet both are so important."

"Go on, Jo. Tell me about the project you have in mind."

"It's not easy to put into words, but I'd like to do a statue which will represent the earth itself. I want to do something that will reveal all the beauty and fruit-fulness of the world and the wonder of creation. I want to—but tell me, does any of this chatter make any sense to you? I must sound like an awful fool!"

"Not at all, Jo," Mr. Kennerley's voice was soft. "You mean that you want to create your own Genesis in stone! Well, I think it's a marvelous idea. In fact, I can't think of a single idea a sculptor could work on that would be better than this one."

Jo grinned. "At any rate, it's good to know you un-derstand. Now all I have to do is find money for the stone to do it in, a model, and she'd better be reason-able, pay the rent for a studio big enough to do such a project in, and then pay rent somewhere else where Yvonne and I can live. And all this has to happen if I have anything left when I've bought my ticket back to France!"

Mr. Kennerley burst into laughter and Jo laughed with him. The problem was nothing at which to laugh, but it was all so mixed up and there was so much of it that it was better to laugh than to cry, which was the only other thing to do. Suddenly, Mr. Kennerley stopped laughing and looked thoughtful. When he finally spoke, what he had to say astounded Jo.

"What would you say, Jo, if I gave you one hun-dred dollars a month for eight months? Then you could go back to France and go to work on your project. Would eight months be enough time? Could you manage then?"

"Could I manage?" For one of the few times in his life, Jo had no words. He could scarcely believe what he had heard! Here was a friend, new found, with whom he had dared discuss a wholly personal problem and this man who knew scarcely anything about him at all was offering to back him for eight months. It was incredible! One could get along fine on a hundred dollars a month, around 1911, especially in France. He shook his head in disbelief.

"Don't you want it, Jo? Won't you take my offer and let me help you?"

"But why? I haven't anything to offer in return! There's no reason for you to come to my rescue like this."

"You're an investment, Jo Davidson! If you succeed in your project, the world is going to be a more beautiful place because of it. Everyone of us has a stake in making the world a better place while we're in it! Do you want me to be cheated of my chance to help?"

And Jo, meeting Mitchell Kennerley's steady gaze saw behind it the trusting nature of a man who loved the world and his own kind. How could he possibly refuse this offer?

Next morning, Jo rose early and bought his ticket back to France—to Yvonne and the project he hadn't believed he'd ever have a chance to do.

"Quite a difference this time," Jo said to Sultan as the boat docked. "Last time I came to Paris, I had a couple of friends, no prospects and no money. Now I have a wife and money to go ahead with a really big piece of work!"

The well-nourished Sultan wagged his shining rope of a tail.

Mr. Kennerly kept his word. People all over France had heard of Jo's New York success and came to commission busts of themselves or members of their families. Then, better than anything else, Yvonne and Jo had a son, Yvon Jacques! How good life is, Jo thought. How could I ever have doubted things would work out?

Now he had the family of his own that he had wanted so much, friends, and his old, faithful Sultan. Besides, he was hard at work on the project, a huge statue called "La Terre" (The Earth).

Perhaps it was well that Jo could never fully believe in his good fortune, for almost as quickly as it began, it very nearly ended.

First Sultan disappeared. Jo searched for him through the streets of Paris, hour after hour, day after day, in sleet and wind, but he never found his pet. Like the toy horse, all the days of his life, Jo never forgot his Sultan, anymore than he ever forgot anyone or anything he had loved.

Then things went badly for Mr. Kennerley and the checks stopped coming regularly. Jo had to give up his studio and the flat Yvonne had kept so attractively. They moved from one place to another, each place less desirable and cheaper than the one before. All the same, each place cost more than Jo could afford.

Once again, Jo found himself spending more and more time away from home, trying to work almost continuously so he could earn enough to keep going. And now it was worse than ever. He realized that before he had only had himself to worry about. Now he had his own family and they were his responsibility.

After a long talk, he and Yvonne decided he should return to America again and try to get another show. But this time Jo refused to go without his family. Despite the struggle for his very existence, he managed to raise enough money for passage to America, once more putting himself deeply into debt.

Back in New York, Mr. Hellman helped Jo find space for another one-man show at another gallery. The central piece of work, of course, was "La

Terre," for in spite of the great difficulties under which he had worked, Jo had accomplished what he set out to do! Hundreds of people came to see Jo's works and everyone seemed to like what they saw, but oddly enough the show failed. It brought few commissions, and all the work, the long trip, the worriment, the debt, was for nothing. For Jo, the worst part of all was that he felt he had failed everyone who believed in him. Now what was he to do? Where could he go? A friend suggested Chicago. Jo thought long and hard about it. He knew he would have to send Yvonne and Jacques back to France, for he realized only too well that he might fail again and living conditions were far more reasonable in Paris.

"Don't mind, Jo," Yvonne comforted him. "You do what you must. We'll be waiting, no matter how things go."

Once again, Jo was parted from his family. This time all his natural confidence nearly vanished. True, this was the life he'd chosen and he must go on with it! Good or bad, success or failure, he had to keep on trying. It was the only possible way he could live with himself.

He bent over the pier rail watching the ship until it was out of sight, as it sailed down New York harbor carrying his family back to France. The gray-brown waters of the Hudson splashed in rhythm against the dock on which he stood. "Between thee and me," the river waves seemed to say, "Me and thee . . ."

Long ago, so Laban had spoken to Jacob, "Mizpah . . . the Lord watch between me and thee, when we are absent, one from another." *A covenant*—a solemn promise, God's seal and blessing upon it!

All the way to Chicago, the train wheels went clack-click-clack between stations and chugg-chugg-chug-g-g-g at the stops, and the sounds seemed to say "Me and thee, thee-and-me," to Jo. Fast or slow, these were the words of the train wheels. Why am I doing this, Jo asked himself? If I failed in New York, what can I possibly hope for in Chicago? At least in New York, I was known! But even as he asked his questions, he knew that their answers were not his to decide.

But try as he would, he couldn't rid himself of worriment over the New York failure and the possible repetition of it in Chicago. For all he knew, maybe he wouldn't even find enough space for a show in this new and strange city. What an awful chance he was taking again! And how lonely he was. How terribly lonely! Now there was no family, no friends, no Sultan to comfort him. And yet as he worried, he couldn't help remembering that there had been other times like this and somehow, someway things had worked out.

Jo registered at a hotel in Chicago, taking one of the cheapest rooms they had. He immediately decided to take a walk and see what this new city was like. He couldn't bear the idea of staying in his small hotel room in this unfamiliar city where he was unknown. Perhaps a walk might help him work out his problems. He had been in such a hurry coming he hadn't done much clear thinking. And so he walked and walked—walked so long his legs became numb, but his eager, observing eyes forgot nothing they looked upon.

Chicago was a busy place, a center point for shipping between East and West. Jo saw mothers and children, hand in hand. In each of them, he saw Yvonne and Jacques. He peered into fine restaurants, handsome houses, splendid shops, all of them well stocked with necessities and luxuries. If only I could afford some of this for my family, he thought! He wandered through the great Marshall Field department store and the busy Carson, Pirie and Scott departments. So much here we could use, he observed, and all I can do is window shop. Jo knew all about window shopping—he had made a game of it years ago as a small boy back on the East Side. He pretended he really did have money and could buy whatever he wished! This or this or even that. The curious thing was that once he imagined he actually was rich, he found he became extremely fussy about how he would spend his money. For example, he might need clothes quite badly at the time, yet when he pretended he had all this wealth, he found fault first with this suit, then with that coat, and would look and look and perhaps not even buy, because nothing would really do. His mother used to tease him about it when she learned about the game.

"Such a funny boy you are, Jo! Money you don't have, but right away let yourself *think* you have, and regular grass is no good anymore. For you it must be a palace and you want it should come with the lawn made of emeralds!"

Jo chuckled to himself now, remembering. Here he was once again—living on wishing and he had already bought—in his mind, of course—a coat of fine imported Australian wool for Jacques and a Pierce-Arrow automobile with gold-plated trim for his mother and an ermine-trimmed bathrobe for Yvonne. How surprised they would all be to receive such fabulous gifts!

Abruptly, Jo frowned and looked at his watch. In exactly one hour, he was due to have an interview with Mr. Gonzales of the Chicago branch of the Reinhardt Galleries. If Mr. Gonzales didn't like the photograph album of Jo's work, there would be no show and no way of even pretending to "window shop" either!

An hour later, Jo sat quietly in Mr. Gonzales' office watching the art director look at the picture album. Would Mr. Gonzales like what he saw there? Would he give Jo a show? Or would this long journey away from all he loved be another failure?

"How much do you charge for doing a bust, Mr. Davidson?" Mr. Gonzales asked unexpectedly, as he studied the pages of the album.

"*Two thousand dollars.*" Jo heard himself say the words and almost gasped with astonishment at his own nerve. Whatever had made him say such a thing? He had never dared charge anything like two thousand dollars in his life! He closed his eyes tightly—he didn't think he could stand looking at Mr. Gonzales' face when Mr. Gonzales would order him out of his office for daring to make such a statement. He went on waiting, eyes closed, but there was complete silence, except for the turning of the album pages. Unable to stand it another second, Jo opened his eyes wide and stared at Mr. Gonzales. But the man wasn't even looking at him! He was completely engrossed in the album. Finally, he closed it, then looked up at Jo and smiled.

"We will be delighted to have you show your works

here in Chicago, Mr. Davidson! How soon can you
be ready?"

Back at his hotel, Jo still couldn't believe it. Two
thousand dollars a bust! And Mr. Gonzales hadn't
been the least bit startled by the figure. It was unbelievable. Two thousand dollars a bust—the things
it would buy for his family! But supposing the show
was a failure, what then? *Oh dear God, what then?*
But even as he asked, Jo knew the answer. There was
a pattern in his coming to Chicago. Always, there
was a pattern, though the pattern was seldom of
man's making. . . .

That night Jo wrote his family about all that happened. He wanted to tell them the show was going
to be a huge success. He didn't know how he knew it,
but he did!

His dreams that night were wondrous and strange.
There were warm coats, beautifully set tables, and
shiny, new automobiles in them. And oh yes—there
was a handsome house too—set in a garden where
the lush green grass was made of emeralds!

As for the show—it was so much of a success that
Jo was not allowed to leave Chicago until he gave
his word he would return and hold another show
there.

Now, for the first time, Jo felt he was well on
the road.

7. Jo's Word

For the next few years, things went smoothly. One day, Walt Kuhn, the young American Jewish artist, known particularly for his paintings of clowns, came to Europe, seeking outstanding artists for a show to be sponsored by the Society of American Painters and

Sculptors. At the time, Jo had already made plans for his own exhibition at the Reinhardt Galleries in New York, and as always, he intended to keep his word to them. Still, he couldn't help getting excited by the ideas Walt had!

"We're going to stage the show at the armory in New York. Twenty-fifth and Lexington. Hundreds of painters and sculptors are going to exhibit and show America what is going on in art today. Why, we're even going to use a little Pine Tree flag the way they did during the American revolution. After all, Jo, *this* art show is an American revolution too!"

"You know I'll help wherever I can, Walt. Maybe I can spare a few of my own pieces for your show, I don't know. But if I can't do anything else, at least let me work at organizing things!"

Busy as he was, Jo helped. The armory show turned out to be a colossal affair. It was estimated that between a hundred thousand to a quarter of a million people came to see it! It was talked about, written about, and still is. Certainly, no one ever expected Art and Artists to make such a stir in an everyday world. But they most surely did!

The exhibition was unlike anything most Americans had ever seen. Colors, forms, ideas were different. People asked how anyone could tell if the pictures were "right side up." Some said kindergarten children painted better. Others thought something was wrong with artists who painted trees and mountains so that they appeared as if made of blocks.

Walt Kuhn had been clever as possible about the display. How well he knew many of the pieces were difficult to understand! The artists who created them might know what they intended, but most of them weren't there and many who were were too shy or found talking difficult.

To avoid difficulty, Walt suggested some of the more unusual pieces be placed next to works such as Jo's—anyone, Walt was certain, could understand what Jo's work meant. Better still, Jo often visited the armory show himself and could easily explain to others not only his own work, but that of those artists unable to speak for themselves. What a man with words Jo was!

"It's outrageous!" a man protested, looking hard at one of the paintings. "Whoever heard of *pink* grass?"

Jo chuckled. "But you knew it was grass, didn't you, sir? It never once occurred to you that it was anything else, now did it?"

The man frowned. "Well, I don't care. I don't like the darn thing anyway!"

"Nobody said you *had* to like it, sir, but if you dislike it, why not dislike it with reason?" Jo thought a moment, then asked, "Have you ever noticed what color the shadows on the snow are?"

The viewer was silent. He was trying hard to remember. Jo knew the man had probably never before bothered to think about such an ordinary thing, although he must have seen it hundreds of times.

"No, I don't think I have," the man admitted. "Do you know?"

"They're purple! The artist looks and sees them so. But so can you! Or anyone else. Just notice next time it snows. Then try to think how it would be if the artist painted snow, making the shadows green. You'd still know they were shadows, wouldn't you?"

"Okay, you win!" the man sighed. "I see your point and you're right!" He smiled, began to turn away, but suddenly turned back and winked at Jo. "You know," he said strongly, "if more artists could explain things as you do, maybe plain people like me wouldn't have so darn much trouble trying to find out what they're up to!"

Jo grinned back. He was happy just knowing one more person would be able to look at a piece of art and try really to understand it.

Now Jo was tasting fame. He fulfilled commissions in the United States, France, and Great Britain as well. In England, he did his first Nobel prize winner,

Rabindranath Tagore, the noted poet of India. (Nobel prizes are awarded annually to those men and women "who, during the preceding year shall have conferred the greatest benefit on mankind.") He also did Israel Zangwill, famous Jewish author. He did Lord Northcliffe, who published several outstanding British newspapers. For once, he was comfortable financially, well able to support his own family and parents and help Yvonne's as well!

In France, in 1914, Jo's second son, Jean, was born. Two sons! How wonderful. But 1914 was an eventful year, not only for Jo, but for the world—for this was the beginning of the First World War.

The war meant financial trouble for Jo again, but he didn't care about that. All he wanted was to help. Never, as long as he lived, was he able to stand by and see something happen to another human being without wanting to do something about it. True, the United States was not yet in this war, but Jo was certain that it would have to be. How could there possibly be a war fought for freedom without America defending it? Long ago, when he had drawn the American flag and eagle on a school blackboard— their meaning had been forever engraved on his spirit. That was why he was so certain America would have to participate.

For safety, he sent his own family to a country

place he had recently purchased in the Pyrenees Mountains. Then he felt free to offer his services as an interpreter or reporter, for by now he spoke both French and German fluently. Unable to secure anything of this sort immediately, he asked Lord Northcliffe to give him a job as an artist-correspondent for the *Daily Mail* and the *London Times*, which Lord Northcliffe published.

"If I can draw pictures of what is happening at the front in this war," he explained, "I may be able to make it clear to the rest of the world what a horrible thing this war really is and why everyone must help."

And so, in Belgium, amid bursting shells and utter destruction, Jo not only drew what he saw so others might see it, but he also served as a translator for an ambulance unit as well. Even this was not enough. He went out with the ambulance unit to help bring back the injured and dead. What he saw, shocked him terribly! It was beyond anything he had ever dared imagine. If only he could show the world with his hands what war meant.

Later, Jo created a gigantic figure, whose original name was "L'Appel Aux Armes" (The Call to Arms). The name was changed to "France Aroused" and a proper name it was, for Jo had made a giant statue of Bellona, Goddess of War. It was a brutal figure and it said coldly, harshly, what such a statue should

say—that war is an outrage, but that the decency in
men must answer and fight that outrage, wherever
it may be. The statue offended many, for most
people still thought war statues should be figures of
heroes and noble ideas. Jo had given them an ugly
figure of tremendous strength and a truth they did
not wish to hear. The statue was rejected. One more
failure, Jo thought, as the figure was moved back into
his studio. Now, what do I do? What is there for
me? For all that in which I believe?

Tucked away in a corner of Jo's mind, there was
an idea, small, but growing. Every once in a while,
it called itself to his attention as if to say, "Now looka-
here, Jo Davidson! Look at me—I'm important!" At
first Jo paid not attention. He was much too busy.
But the tiny idea became full grown and could no
longer be ignored.

Jo had done many busts by now, some by order,
some at his own request. Many were outstanding
because they were more than mere craft. They were
also history. With a war so great going on, Jo was
more aware than ever of history, of the changes
that keep taking place in the lives of people everywhere.

At first, the small idea had been to sculpture people
whom he found interesting—whom he liked, who
liked him. But as the idea grew, Jo saw that the liking

part didn't matter particularly. What did matter was to "bust" the people who were responsible for affecting the lives of others. What kind of people are these who can make others live as they wish? How do they act? What do they look like?

Yes, the idea was now immense. So big it was hard to know where to begin! Jo thought about it carefully before he went ahead. He decided he would do as many busts of important people of his times as he could. He would have to forget his own feelings about liking them and remember only to reveal them as plainly as he could, no matter how much he might dislike their ideas. He remembered how Israel Zangwill had said when his bust was finished that there was nothing new about his work, that all Jo had done was to display his own hunger for truth.

"But my sculpture *is* new. It has more than form! It has movement and—"

"Nonsense!" Zangwill had cut Jo short. "You have what I have—a passion for truth, even when it's unpleasant. Sometimes I think it's the most Jewish thing about me. And you have it too, whether or not you realize it!" He winked at Jo and touched the bust of himself. "Take my mouth now. You could have made it smaller, but you didn't. My chin isn't nearly as strong as I thought it was and I seem to be too stern. I'm not the least bit handsome and something tells

me that down underneath anyone who looks at my
bust is going to see that I fret too much. You saw it
all and you put it in, good and bad together. And
there it stands—the truth!"

Jo smiled, almost shyly. "Then tell me, Mr. Zangwill, do you like your bust?"

Zangwill grinned. "I like it very much. It says the
truth about me, and as I told you—I have a passion
for the truth!"

What he had done in Zangwill's bust, Jo had
in mind now for the rest of the men who "make"
the world what it is. A plastic history! He had already
done Tagore, Northcliffe, Zangwill and many others
and they would fit in well with his plan, but what
a gigantic job it was going to be. And yet, if he
succeeded, the world would have an unforgettable
heritage!

The war meant little work for Jo to do, so that
he had to live on his previous earnings. Now, once
more he was broke. Once more, he turned to his
many friends. He told them of his idea and several
of them agreed on its importance, to the extent of
lending him money, which Jo accepted and used to
book passage for America. There he hoped to do
the President of the United States, Woodrow Wilson,
truly one of the great men of the world!

Jo's house had been turned into a hospital for the

injured and dying and Yvonne worked from early morning to late at night, trying to help. Despite the fact that things were rather difficult for both of them, they both understood that Jo had to carry on with his idea. They knew too that much of what Jo wanted to do was going to have to be done without payment. Once again it would mean that Jo would live in one part of the world while Yvonne lived in another. Still, it had to be done! Jo burned with ambition for the immense job he had set himself.

He wondered what it would be like to sculpture the President of the United States—and in particular, this President. For Woodrow Wilson was one of the most brilliant and revered men in the world! But when Jo finally arrived in America, nothing went according to plan. At first, the President was most unwilling to have his bust done. With everything else he had to do, how could he possibly take time out to sit for a bust? Besides, why was it so important? People were always taking pictures of him and that ought to be enough! It took much convincing and a final push from the Democratic Party itself before the President agreed.

Wilson had been a professor at Princeton University before he had been elected, first to the governorship of New Jersey, then to the presidency of the United States. There was no question about it—he was doubtlessly one of the most intellectual presidents the nation ever had. Until the time of Wilson, most Americans believed firmly that the Atlantic and Pacific Oceans were quite large enough to separate us forever from the troubles of the rest of the world! Wilson knew otherwise. He believed that the hope of the world rested in all the people getting together and working for the benefit of all. Eventually, his plan produced a "League of Nations," which—although it tried hard—was never too successful. At the time Jo did his bust, early in 1916, America was not yet in World War I. While Jo sculptured President Wilson, he dared to bring up the subject!

"But, Mr. President, how can our country possibly stay out of this war? If we believe what we say we do, then we must fight!"

"I am the *servant* of the people, Mr. Davidson." President Wilson answered gravely. "That is the capacity of the President of the United States. When and if the people of this nation feel it is time to enter this war, then they shall order me to do so. Till then, I wait on them!"

Before the year was out, the people of the United States made that demand and President Wilson carried the mission through with total success! In his efforts to achieve peace, Wilson earned the Nobel prize.

In Jo's bust of Wilson, now in the library at Princeton University, the viewer looks into the face of a man who is at once fighter and dreamer, a man whose ideas are generations ahead of his own time. The photographs people took of him seem, without exception, to show a cold, dignified man, but Jo's bust reveals an inner fire that could not be quenched. Here was a man who believed men might achieve heaven before they had even learned how to lift their feet out of the mud! It was this man that Jo saw and sculptured!

Before the Peace Conference at the end of the war was over, Jo was back in France and had sculptured many of the leading men of the countries involved. He did Marshall Foch, Commander-in-Chief of the Allied Forces, Lord Arthur James Balfour, great friend of the Jewish people, who represented, together with Lloyd George, the British claims, and also Georges Clemenceau, known as "The Tiger," who had led France to victory.

During this period, Jo did the bust of the "Eisenhower" of World War I, General Pershing. It was while working on General Pershing's bust that Jo noticed a young soldier at his headquarters whom Jo felt was a representation of every American boy who had fought in the war. He succeeded in making a 16-foot statue of the young man, which he did on a commission of the widow of an officer who had died in the war. It was her wish to place this magnificent figure in an American cemetery, but when the project was done, despite all the plans that had been made, there was no place for it! For more than ten years, Jo kept it in his studio. It was only when the city of Paris decided to cut a street through Jo's workrooms, that Jo was forced to part with this fine work. He had no way of raising enough money to move such a huge piece.

Sorrowfully, he took the statue apart, carefully severing each section, for huge statues are made in many sections, although the viewer is seldom aware of it, so carefully are they put together. As the last piece fell, Jo held it close to him. It meant something dear to him, in which he had firmly believed, and now it had come to this. Gently, he put it down with the rest of the parts—parts, which together, had been a work of great scope and power, and now would never mean anything at all.

He walked quickly out of the studio, closing the door forever behind him. He knew, without having to ask, that it had not all been useless. Everything he had learned in making the statue of the soldier would go into new and perhaps even more important things. Who could tell what was waiting for him now?

8. The Twenties

The twenties were amazing years. For the first time, the results of an American election were broadcast over the radio—the election of President Warren G. Harding. Charles Augustus Lindberg, "Lucky Lindy," in a single-engine Ryan airplane made the *first* nonstop solo flight between New York and Paris. A young Austrian corporal was beginning to band together a group of rowdies in Germany. His name was Adolph Hitler. Anatole France and Albert Einstein won Nobel prizes in the same year, 1921. George Bernard Shaw did it in 1925. A young writer, Sinclair "Red" Lewis, a Midwesterner, was startling the world with his books about small-town American life. The twenties were years of money and fun, "a time for laughter." But the end of the twenties was the beginning of a depression which would mean huge manufacturing plants would close their doors for years. Thousands of people would be jobless, with no hope of getting work, standing in line for the free bread and soup distributed by charities.

But now, in the twenties, Jo was at his busiest.

For Jo, Anatole France had once been only the sketch of a man on the drawing board of a newspaper artist. In 1921, Jo met him, through a mutual friend, and did his head in bronze. Even while France sat for him, Jo had a hard time realizing it was really happening. As a boy, Jo had dreamed great dreams, but it takes more than dreaming to make them come true. Yet here was Anatole France, sitting for him.

In doing his sculpture, Jo used an armature of his own design. An armature is usually a special wire structure, around which the sculptor molds his forms.

Jo had designed his with a key in the back, so that as a model spoke, or moved, just that fast—only as long as it took to turn that key—he could shape the entire head into the same position as his model assumed. Other artists had to have a model sit in a definite position before they could proceed, but Jo had his own ideas about that. What mattered to him was that he "caught" his people just as they were, the way they tilted their head or lowered it, their smiles, their grimaces, and the key in that armature held part of his secret. The rest was in himself, and that was the greater part, of course.

While Anatole France posed, Jo told him how, as a boy working for a newspaper, he had watched the artists draw pictures to go with the reports on the trial of Captain Alfred Dreyfus.

Dreyfus was the first Jew ever named to the French General Staff. When he was arrested, charged with treason, all France was seized with almost blood-thirsty panic. It was later proved that Dreyfus had been falsely accused, but in the meantime his enemies made the most of the fact that the entire affair would never have occurred if a Jew hadn't been involved.

Emile Zola and Anatole France, two men at the height of their professions as writers, came to the defense of Dreyfus.

"It was a remarkably brave thing to have done,"

Jo said to France as he worked on his bust, "for after all, it almost destroyed Dreyfus and it brought exile to Zola. It might well have ruined you too."

"Because one's life is threatened, there is no reason to keep silent about injustice." France spoke calmly.

"Others have found it reason enough. After all, the Dreyfus case nearly caused a civil war, didn't it?"

France shrugged. Jo understood then that he would do the same thing all over again, if he ever felt it necessary. The books Anatole France had written were fine in craftsmanship, witty, and often satires on human thinking. But always beneath, there was an unmistakable awareness of righteousness and a genuine affection for people.

France was a man who loved beautiful things, who lived in an exquisite house, and who dressed with careful attention to detail. His face was brooding, rich in outward beauty, as the mind which lay behind it. Yet much as he loved beauty, Jo saw in him a man who would not have hesitated to sacrifice everything he had, for what he believed in. It is no accident that the bust of Anatole France is one of Jo's best works!

In Jo's imagination when he had not yet made that first trip to Paris to study, he often thought he might someday be a visitor in the studios of Gertrude Stein and her brother, Leo. Writers and artists of all kinds visited Gertrude's apartment. Whenever people spoke about art movements or new writing, Gertrude's name was mentioned.

She had been born in Pennsylvania of American Jewish parentage, raised in California, educated in American universities, but she had left her native country to settle permanently in Paris.

Her physical appearance was "a natural" for artists and sculptors. She was fat, her body full as a bed-pillow with a string around the middle for a waist-line. Her features were sharp, strong, her expression alert. For many years, she wore her head topped by a bun, then she cut it quite short so it looked like a child's first haircut. No wonder her appearance was so fascinating to artists!

"I'd like to sculpture you, Gertrude," Jo said one day after they had met and become friends. "Oh yes, I know others have done you, but I think my version may turn out differently from all the rest!"

"I don't like posing." Gertrude frowned. "I find it a dreadful bore."

"Perhaps you won't mind it so much this time. Wait and see!"

So Gertrude Stein sat for Jo. While she posed, she read some of her writing to him. One day she brought along only a single sentence! She read it over and

over in as many ways as she could. The sentence became famous, and Gertrude's companion, Alice B.
Toklas, thought it was a fine motto for Gertrude, so
she embroidered it on tablecloths, napkins, and bed-
linens. The sentence was, "A rose is a rose is a rose."
Alice made the sentence into a circle and embroidered
it going round and round and round.

The sentence might have had many meanings, of
course. One is that a thing is what it is and nothing
can change it. But the important thing about the
sentence is that it gives a good idea of what made
Gertrude's writing so easy to read and so hard to
understand!

Jo decided not to do a bust of Gertrude. He
thought the only proper way to "do" her was to do
all of her. After all, that was how she tried to write,
putting all of her ideas in a thing at one time.

When he had finished, his statue was a large, sitting
figure, which looked—as Jo's friend, Lincoln Steffens,
remarked, like a giant Buddha. Jo was a little worried
about how Gertrude would feel about this work, for
she was quite shrewd, and although her ideas were
sometimes hard to understand in writing, her mind
understood just about everything.

"It's all finished, Gertrude. Would you like to see
it?"

Gertrude arose and walked all around herself. First

she walked clockwise, then she walked counterclockwise.

"You've done it, Jo. I can look at that and say, 'That's Gertrude Stein, that's all of Gertrude there is.'"

"A Gertrude is a Gertrude is a Gertrude!" Jo teased.

Gertrude burst into laughter at Jo's sentence about her. But everyone who sees Jo's statue of Gertrude can say as he did that "A Gertrude is a Gertrude is a Gertrude," even as she had once written, "A rose is a rose is a rose." Nobody since or before, except Jo Davidson, even really did *all* of Gertrude Stein!

Gertrude was so pleased she wrote an article about Jo which appeared in a magazine called *Vanity Fair*. Unfortunately neither Jo nor his friends, understood what Gertrude was saying about him. Still, it didn't matter much because if anyone really wanted to understand Gertrude, the statue Jo had done was there and even without words it explained everything there was to know about Gertrude Stein.

Things continued to happen rapidly in the twenties. All sorts of new inventions and events. A huge ship, the H.M.S. *Hermes*, was being built in England and there was a rumor that it would carry airplanes, which could be launched directly from the deck! A big show was held in America in which all sorts of things made possible with electricity were shown. People discussed the possibility that perhaps some day there would even be such an item as electric razors!

"Not for me!" Jo laughed, when he heard it. "This beard of mine is an old friend, though I'll admit it bothers the dickens out of me in hot weather. But electric razors or not, it stays put."

Once the hot weather had been too much and he had shaved it off. Afterwards, although he spent the day walking the same streets and visiting the same places he always did, none of his friends had recognized him. And when he went home that evening, Jacques and Jean thought him a stranger and were frightened. Only Yvonne recognized him.

"Jo Davidson, you let that beard grow right back!" she scolded. "Even your own family didn't recognize you!"

So the beard had been grown again and stayed permanently.

Not everything that had happened since the end of the war had been happy for Jo. One event was tragic—his beloved mother, Haya, died.

She had been to the store shopping. It was a lovely day, the sky an inviting blue, and the streets were filled with the sounds of children at play, calling to one another, and when it was time to come in— their mothers calling to them.

Haya smiled a little, remembering how Jo had always played in the streets on such days as this and how she had called him "Jo-*eey!*" Ach, those were the good days! True, there had never been much money and the boy had had to work hard, but he had been there with her. How happy they all were when they heard his voice, his merry laughter! Memories flooded her heart. She saw him so rarely these days. Most of the time he lived and worked in France, yet far away as he was, he never forgot her. Not only had he sculptured the President of the United States, but he had bravely sailed the seas filled with enemy ships and submarines to do the busts of other great leaders.

"My head too, he did!" she murmured. "My head. Imagine it. Always, I said, 'Jo—he's *my* sculptor'! Now he's *everybody's* sculptor! Eighty years old I am. How many other mothers have had so much from their children? If only his father could have lived to see it all. '*My* sculptor!' "

Jo's father, Jacob, had died in 1910, while Jo was traveling from France. Haya recalled how upset Jo had been, arriving too late, his father already buried, the Kaddish said. She had consoled him.

"It's all right, son. If your father had lived, he would have understood. It was God's will, and your father was never one to question the will of God."

Eighty years had caressed Haya's face with sweetness. Her laughter still rang clear and free, her trust in her children and her faith had never been disturbed.

Content now in her remembrance of that other day, so many years ago, Haya did not see what was happening in the street where she walked. The youngsters were playing handball and the one up at bat swatted the ball, sending it far down the street. Instantly, he began to run and Haya was directly in his path! Neither of them knew exactly what happened. Moments later, Haya's crumpled form lay at the boy's feet, one leg turned inward at a peculiar angle.

"My hip, my hip . . ." she moaned, gasping in pain.

For all the new things happening in 1923, the proper care of a broken hip in an aged person was not yet known. There was little to be done and to add to the difficulty, pneumonia set in. Before word could reach Jo, Haya was gone.

In Paris, Jo threw aside his chisel on hearing the news, unable to continue working. He was a man grown to full stature and greatness, but in this moment he was once more the small boy who had changed his name and taken the legs off a toy horse. Now he was well traveled, well known, and he spoke several languages fluently. Yet the words he had need of now were ancient Hebrew words and in his heart, he said them.

When at last he was able to return to his work, he knew that as long as he lived, the spirit of his mother would never depart.

Later that year, Jo went to Russia with the senator from Wisconsin, Robert LaFollette. Jo had always wanted to go to Russia, even as any American may sometimes want to go to the country from which his people have come.

President Dwight D. Eisenhower once said, "We are one and all immigrants and the sons and daughters of immigrants," and that is true. Nearly every American has some sort of sentimental interest in another country. In Jo's case, it was Russia. Hadn't his mother told him all sorts of stories about her life there? She had made them so interesting he thought it quite possible that he might even be able to pick out the tree under which she had once sat. Besides, the Russian Revolution was over now and a new kind of history was being made there. Where else does a historian belong if not where history is happening?

So Jo made his first trip to Russia. Earlier, while in Genoa, he had met some of the leaders of the new Russian government at a meeting there. He had found them a terribly serious people, preferring to have

around them only those sympathetic to their ideas.
Jo enjoyed good conversation, food—and more,
laughter. He realized these people had not yet learned
that laughter is one of man's most precious gifts—particularly his own laughter at himself!

For all of that, Jo knew it was important for the
world to have as true a picture of these people with
their plans as was possible, for indeed many of their
plans were for the rest of the world as well as themselves. He made as many busts of them as he could
and he left careful instructions concerning the shipping of these pieces. Despite all his precautions, only
one bust arrived in his Paris studio unbroken, and even
that one was badly damaged. And yet, he was far less
disappointed at the sight of that broken work of
months than he was at the broken dream he had that
even a small part of Russia might still have remained
the way his mother had told him it was in her stories.

In 1924, back in America, Jo did his first bust of
John D. Rockefeller, by reputation America's richest
man. He stayed at Rockefeller's house while he
worked, learning about his character, not only from
observing while he worked on his bust, but from actually living with him day in, day out. Rockefeller
was eighty-five then, an old man, but still active.
People were talking, just as they always had, about

Rockefeller and his money. Somehow, they never seemed able to separate the two! Jo heard many of the stories and listened without opinion. He would learn for himself what was true and what wasn't, and what he found was what he would show!

Rockefeller's middle name was Davison. His secretary's name was *Davis*. He liked the idea that his sculptor would be Davi*d*son! He sat patiently, not seeming to mind it at all, despite his age. He had a fund of amusing stories which he told Jo as he worked.

Jo found his manner strange in a way things are strange when they seem to belong to another time. Rather like going to a museum, seeing all the furniture and utensils people once used, then trying to imagine how your grandparents looked when these things were in fashion. Yet you're certain grandmother and grandfather couldn't possibly be *that* old! But still, they must have been. . . . And here was Rockefeller telling you exactly how things were then, for his memory was remarkable and he knew what had happened yesterday, was happening today, might even happen tomorrow. He realized he was hated and feared. No man who has ever possessed so much of the world's wealth has failed to know that. Some have accepted it as a sign of power, some have guarded themselves against it. Jo realized all it had done for Rockefeller was to make him grieve. He had vast treasure, but he also had vast conscience. He believed if you amassed tremendous money you must try, if you could, to do as much good with it as possible. That, Rockefeller firmly believed, was the meaning of money—to be used for a good purpose and he tried his best.

Rockefeller founded the great University of Chicago. In 1913, he gave to various charities approximately five hundred million dollars! Some of this was used to establish the Rockefeller Foundation, set up "to promote public health and further science." The Foundation has continued to try and follow what its founder believed, helping mankind all over the world.

By the time Jo finished Rockefeller's bust, he knew he had seen and lived with a man, lonely in wealth, firm in belief, who wanted to do good and did it in the only way he knew.

Jo's bust shows the old gentleman, who at one time had suffered such severe illness that he had lost hair, eyebrows and lashes. His hair had come back scantily, but his lashes were sparse to the point of not seeming to exist, so that his eyes gave an impression of peering into some far-off world. It was almost as if Rockefeller was using the unique foresightedness which had made his fortune, to see into the world of the future, a world which he had tried to make better.

When he died at ninety-seven, Rockefeller's mind was still sharp, and his hearing good. He lived to see much of what he planned do the good he had intended.

Jo's bust pleased him immensely, for it neither flattered nor ridiculed. Jo had indeed "done" Rockefeller *without* his money. And Rockefeller *without* his money was even so an imposing and wise figure.

He asked Jo to make a duplicate bust, which may be seen in the Standard Oil Building in New York. The original bust was done in marble, but for the duplicate, which is quite large, Jo chose a stone from France. He seemed to feel that this particular stone was extremely well suited to reveal Rockefeller, for oddly it had a warm flesh tone—almost as if it was meant to reveal clearly the man whom most people had thought of as only having money.

These years Jo was excessively active and he hired several assistants. One of them, Gino, worked and spent his life with Jo. Others went on their way to outstanding success of their own. All remembered him with affection and pleasure.

He was important enough these days to "pick" those whom he wished to pose for him.

"It's grand to have money," he told Yvonne, "because it allows you to do many things you've always wanted to do. But the thing to remember is that these things must be important! I must keep on with my plastic history whether or not I'm paid for it. I'm going to show my world as it is, money or not."

Yvonne no longer agreed. "That's fine, Jo, but now that you are successful, why not experiment with another art form?" She was thinking in terms of more modern art, which many of the people whom they knew were doing. The world was beginning to accept some of these others, beginning to get used to finding humor as well as machinery and geometric forms and splotches. Sculpture had assumed strange shapes. Much of it, even when not understood, was supposed to be fine art!

"After all, Jo, art can be many things. Ideas, dreams, moods. You know that even better than I!"

Jo sighed. He knew what Yvonne meant. When they had first married, sometimes he had moved along so fast that he had been too rapid for Yvonne, but as he grew older and saw more of the world in which he lived, he grew wiser and his feelings changed with his thinking. He had secretly tried some of the newer forms so that he knew he could do them, but something held him back. People meant too much to him! What others did might be right for them, but he saw people differently. They were too important to him to reveal himself instead of them in what he did.

"I'm sorry, Yvonne. I can't."

"But Jo, with your ability, you could do something altogether striking!"

Jo bit his lip. Yvonne had become quite successful as a dress designer and was well known everywhere. But fashion designing wasn't Jo's idea of art and many of his fellow artists seemed to think, like fashion designers, that their work had to be one step ahead of tomorrow to be any good. He wished he could make Yvonne see what he meant.

Maybe, he thought, when I did Charlie Chaplin, the comedian, I shouldn't have done his face. Just a funny mustache, a cane, and turned up shoes, and called it "Chaplin." My "David" could have been a strong young arm and a slingshot. These are *striking* ideas, but they're not for me!

"If you are right, Yvonne," he said slowly, "then when I sculpture a writer, all I need is a book, a pen, and a few bizarre angles. A long beard if it's Anatole France, or a shape like a flourbag if it's Gertrude Stein. Who, besides me, will know the difference? Aren't they both writers?"

"Jo! You know that's not what I meant at all!"

"Perhaps not. But I'm doing the people of my world as they are! No matter how many cubes, angles, eyes, or my own impressions I may put in, these people are still individuals, the way God made them. It's like saying the juice of the orange is *all* the orange there is, when I know that's not true at all. No, Yvonne, this stuff is not for me!"

Yvonne was silent. She knew there was no changing his mind.

Inwardly, Jo was disturbed. He realized that Yvonne was tactfully trying to tell him he was somewhat old-fashioned. Well, so he would continue! Weren't people old-fashioned? Didn't they keep getting born into the world in the same old-fashioned way? And their hearts beat in the same old-fashioned rhythm. God himself, he thought knowingly, is old-fashioned too! No, he would go on as he had.

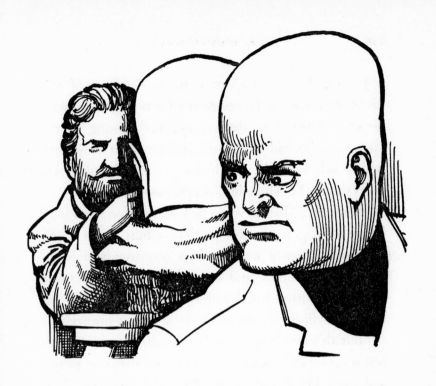

9. Jo and the Dictator

In the middle twenties, in Italy, Benito Mussolini had already succeeded in becoming a full-fledged dictator. No one who has ever seen a picture of Mussolini with the shaven skull, the burning eyes, the set mask of a face, could forget him. But what was he really like? How did Jo see him?

Jo considered it important to do the bust of this dictator because he represented a form of government, directly opposed to democracy, yet existing at the same time. Jo had been born and raised in a country which believed what he believed—that people were everything. To Mussolini, people were nothing.

"Someday," Jo said when he was questioned on why he was going to do this particular bust, "this man's ideas may mean a war between countries which believe in democracy and countries which keep their people downtrodden. Unpleasant though it may be, this man will have a definite part in such a history."

"But this man is supposed to be dangerous! Everyone is afraid of him. He has had men thrown in prison and even killed for the smallest disagreements. You may be taking a terrible risk!"

"If I call myself a historian, then I have no choice. Whether or not I like what Mussolini represents, I still know he must be part of my history."

So Jo went ahead with his arrangements to do Mussolini's bust in the dictator's own offices in Rome.

"You'll understand I'm an extremely busy man!" Mussolini informed him. "I'm not to be interrupted, so you'll just have to work on my bust while I settle important affairs of state!"

"Go right ahead with whatever you have to do," Jo answered calmly, for he always asked everyone to go ahead and do the work they usually did. "I'll manage fine. Later on, I may need a few moments alone with you."

"I'll give you whatever time I can spare, but don't ask for too much! I'm tremendously important to *my* government. You may not know it, but I hold seven top positions. Nothing around here can run without me!"

Jo swallowed hard, but did not comment. War-maker, he thought. But history would not be history without the picture of such a man. Evil or not, he must be included.

Jo worked on Mussolini's bust as well as he could under the circumstances. Mussolini was constantly "on the go." People came in and out of his office for interviews, reports, to pay tribute with words and flowers, medals, elaborate gifts. And almost everyone who entered was terrified of him. Men known for heroism in physical combat against the worst kind of danger were sometimes so frightened in Mussolini's presence that they were afraid to raise their eyes and look at him directly. Why are all of them so frightened, Jo wondered? He studied his subject carefully.

"Even if I weren't around to do his bust," Jo told some of his friends, "Mussolini would pose. That's all he ever does—pose. Constantly. He's nothing but a big bluff."

"Sh-h!" his friends cautioned Jo. "You mustn't let anyone hear you say such things. He's so dangerous that if he even heard part of what you said he'd make certain you'd disappear from the face of the earth!"

"Nonsense!" Jo retorted. "I still say he's a big bluff and I don't care if he hears it or not!"

The work went more slowly than most of Jo's assignments. His model was never still, never relaxed. Jo asked him for a little time alone.

"I'll give you ten or fifteen minutes," Mussolini agreed. "Then you can do one side of my face and go ahead with the rest!"

"I'm going to need more time than that. Both sides of your face aren't the same! Nobody's is."

"Well, *my* face is! Both sides exactly alike!" Mussolini struck another pose. It made him look a little like the pictures Jo had seen of Napoleon.

"Let me show you," Jo tried explaining. "I'll prove to you what I mean."

"Oh, I'll grant there may be a small difference," Mussolini stuck out his lower lip in a well-known pout. "But in my case it couldn't possibly amount to anything much. I've looked in my mirror often enough to know!"

I'll bet you have, Jo thought in amusement. You act as if you're looking at yourself in a mirror all day long! But he realized it was useless to try to reason with this man. Mussolini would believe only what he wished to believe.

The sessions continued with Mussolini striking poses constantly and Jo trying desperately hard to get what he knew he must—a pose from the *inside* of this dictator.

One day Jo could stand it no longer. Mussolini was close by him that particular day, his head constantly moving, his voice rasping out unceasing demands, his hands gesturing. Suddenly, Jo reached out and grasped the dictator's shaven skull and held it firmly! Mussolini was so startled by Jo's action that he was speechless. He gasped, looked sidewise at Jo, but there was no mistaking it. Jo Davidson meant business! He went right on holding Mussolini's head until he had what he wanted . . .

After that incident, the dictator's bust was completed according to Jo's wishes.

Back at his hotel packing to go home, Jo chuckled at what had happened. Nobody really needed to have any trouble at all with this dictator. All they had to do was grab his shaven head and hold on to it.

"I'm glad my first piece of work was young David," he said, not caring whether anyone heard him or not. "It gave me the feeling then of what you have to do to kill a Goliath. No wonder David was unafraid. Goliath was probably a big bluff too."

10. The Thirties

The thirties too meant many changes. In the thirties, people knew unemployment, bank failures, old age without any ability to protect themselves against poverty or illness. The thirties saw new laws enacted to protect Americans against these disasters.

In the thirties too, the world saw the emergence of a strong American president, Franklin Delano Roosevelt, the first president to stay in office not only two successive terms, but three, and almost four. Roosevelt played a major role in Jo's life.

In the thirties, as in the twenties, Jo was extremely busy. History unfolded at a fierce pace. In India, an ugly brown man, who wore only a piece of white cloth, which he had woven himself, and thin sandals, was fighting to set his entire nation free by not fighting at all. He had the idea that the greatest fighting done was with love and peace. He trained his people in the knowledge that it takes more courage to take a beating than to give one. When he came to London in 1931 to plead for his people, Jo made one of his most remarkable sculptures of this strange and great man, Mahatma Gandhi.

In this decade too, Jo was to know great sorrow in his own life, but the thirties began well for him and ended with two works, which—had he never done anything else in his lifetime—would have been enough to establish him as one of the greatest sculptors who ever lived.

In 1930, George Doran, then a member of a well-known book publishing firm, asked Jo to do a series of busts of well-known authors whose books were published by his company. Jo was enthusiastic about the idea. Next to looking at people and talking to them, Jo loved books. He felt that writers often had such impact upon people that their lives were guided by something they happened to read. Many of the writers Doran suggested had been Nobel prize winners.

Jo added other writers to Mr. Doran's list. These included Sir James Barrie, whose "Peter Pan" no child ever forgets, George Bernard Shaw, whom many people rate as "the twentieth century Shakespeare," and James Joyce, who wrote in an even more difficult and masterly fashion than Gertrude Stein, as well as H. G. Wells, the father of science-fiction stories.

These figures were exhibited in a show in 1932—a show overwhelming in its success. In rooms filled with these and other figures Jo had sculpted, the impression was one of awe, not only at the force of the models themselves, but at the vast, almost incredible understanding and energy of the man who had done them. It was astounding that one human being should have in him not only such artistic ability, but what was greater —a comprehension and physical endurance so intense that he could reveal completely an entire world with the magic of his mind and hands. Yvonne was overcome by sudden awareness of Jo's genius.

"Oh, Jo, Jo!" she said over and over, "I had no idea. No idea at all!"

And Jo, friendly as a child, accepted her praise gratefully. He had been sure she would understand and now she had!

The bust which drew most of the attention, however, was the one Jo had done of Roosevelt, the man on whom not only his own country, but the entire world looked to lead the people out of the depression years of the thirties.

From the first the President and the sculptor had gotten on together. One might have thought they were old friends.

"You're from New York State, Mr. President?"

Mr. Roosevelt appraised Jo shrewdly. "Born there in 1882, and although that beard of yours makes it a little hard to tell, I'd say we're about the same age."

"A year apart!" Jo laughed. "Lower East Side New York in 1883, Mr. President. And I'll make a bet too. I'd say that although we came up by different routes, we both had to learn the same things the hard way."

The President's face saddened. Unconsciously, he reached down and touched his braced legs, withered from a vicious attack of polio he had suffered as a grown man. Until then, things had been rather easy for him, but pain had taught him much—even as a different kind of suffering had taught Jo the things he knew.

Once Roosevelt had been a healthy, active man, able to do all the things anyone else did—and more. Then he had been crippled for life. He had fought his disease valiantly, learning how to walk with the aid of braces and crutches, then braces and a cane, but always needing someone's help to move properly. The President had an unsatisfied hunger to stand free, but he had been forced to learn that never again would he be able to, that something most everyone else took for granted was something he could never hope for again. Very well then, he made up his mind. If his legs weren't free, his mind was—and his mind was far more important than his legs. With his mind, perhaps he could help others even less fortunate to stand free in their own fashion.

One of the things Jo liked best about Roosevelt, however, was that he not only tried hard to bring order out of chaos, but that he remembered—as did no president before him—that artists of all kinds are important to the wealth of a nation. When later generations measure the civilization of any period, they consider its culture as a guide. Roosevelt was wise enough to understand this.

"Roosevelt's a President for *all* the people!" Jo told friends. "Maybe he won't succeed. He's bound to be disliked by people who believe in nothing but self-preservation, but no one will ever be able to come along and say he didn't try to teach them that they should think of others as well."

"You're an idealist, Jo," a friend teased. "Imagine an idealist getting interested in a politician."

"But it isn't that. It's simply that I think we have a president who is doing his utmost to help people. He needs all the support he can get to do it. He's probably known more suffering than most of us have in a lifetime and he never has a minute in which to forget it. Yet he goes right on trying to help."

President Roosevelt warned Jo about trying to back up some of his ideas.

"I appreciate your feelings, Jo," he said matter-of-factly, "but politics is nasty business. No matter how hard you try to do the right thing, there are always people around who think you're trying to do exactly the opposite." He was silent before going on. "Besides, Jo, there's bound to be name-calling too. Is it worth it?"

"I've been called names before, Mr. President," Jo said knowingly. "It's something my people know all about. It's only a little pain for a little while." He lowered his voice, adding gently, "Is it worth it to *you?*"

"Mine is only physical pain." The President's voice was courageous. "Anyone can rise above *that!*"

But Jo knew that Roosevelt suffered more than

physical pain—that he had won the long, hard fight against the mental defeat that such continuous pain could mean.

The head Jo did of Roosevelt was that of a man in whom every outline says, "Courage! We shall find a way." And somehow the viewer sensed no matter how impossible the problem, here was a man who could meet and conquer it!

Jo had two homes in France now, both of which he had had for a number of years. One was in the South of France, a lovely rolling country site, which he called "Becheron." The other was in Paris. Still, he remained American, making trips back and forth until it seemed as if there must be a ferry boat running between America and Europe just for him.

On one visit, he had done the head of an Oklahoma oil man, Mr. Marland, who insisted Jo see the rest of his native country. It was then that Jo had fallen in love all over again with his own land. Now, in 1934, after his great one-man show, he wanted to take another trip across country to the West Coast and back, this time with Yvonne accompanying him. She had not been feeling well and Jo was positive the change would do her good. Besides, they could stop in California and see his sister, Rose, who lived in Carmel with her professor-husband.

The trip was delightful, what with Jo painting water-colors of all the scenery he saw from the train, using a miniature paint box which he had found in a New York shop. The box was quite tiny, only one by two inches, but complete, and Jo would slip it into his pocket so that it was always ready for work. As Jo anticipated, Yvonne was happy on the trip and seemed to relax and feel better. They spent slow, lazy days and nights visiting relatives and friends and Jo even made some busts en route. He was certain that the sky of his world was a clear, cloudless blue, without a storm in sight. Yvonne was much improved and ready to return to France. But back in their New York hotel room, their passage to France ready, Yvonne suddenly complained of feeling dreadfully ill and collapsed. In less than a week, she was dead!

Jo took Yvonne home to France and buried her in Becheron. Her death overwhelmed him and things no longer seemed to have any meaning for him. His sons were now grown men and could stand on their own. He felt as if he were all alone in a world which had no need of him at all! Then, in memory of Yvonne, he began to make an exquisite figure of a resting girl, which he placed in the garden at Becheron. In doing this work, he began once more to feel a new-found surge of strength in himself. When he finished, he looked at the lovely form he had made and realized

life was not over for him at all. He could still work
and work well. Oddly enough, what he touched now
seemed altogether new! It was almost as if the tears he
had wept for Yvonne had become molded in his clay,
enriching whatever he touched with something holy.

Another sculpture Jo did after Yvonne's death was
a bust of Albert Einstein. Here again was a meeting
that resulted in great understanding, for Einstein and
Jo, although they were entirely different in the work
they did, had many things in common.

For one thing, Einstein, like Jo, had spent the days
of his life in a world where Jews and non-Jews mingled closely, working together for a common good.
For another, Einstein had once been so desperately
poor that in order to earn money to continue his
studies, he had posed for artists!

Perhaps that was why he didn't mind posing for Jo,
although he found Jo's ability to sense what was "inside" people as difficult as Jo found mathematics! Like
Jo, too, although he had spent his life in a field among
men of many different creeds and nationalities, his
thinking was essentially Jewish.

Einstein was striking in appearance, his hair dark in
youth becoming a silver mane as he grew older. He
was seldom without a pipe, which he drew upon as if

it was a particular treat someone had thought up just for him. He had taught himself to play the violin and played it astonishingly well. A man of gentleness, who loved children deeply, and who knew anger but rarely —what a figure this was for Jo to do!

No one knew better than Einstein or Jo that the Jewish mind is a mind, which set free from persecution, may bring achievement wherever it abides. Such a contribution Einstein made to science and Jo Davidson to art.

Jo told Einstein he would like to do his bust while the scientist worked as he generally did—on extraordinarily difficult calculations at the Institute for Advanced Study at Princeton University.

When Jo entered the room where Doctor Einstein was seated, his first impression was of the face of the visionary, oddly surrounded by blackboards on which were written incomprehensible symbols and numbers.

"How strange," Jo mused, "to think both of us have sprung from one common source!"

The finished bust shows the reflective, gentle face of that man of vast vision, a face as generous in its outlines as the hair which flowed as naturally from the noble forehead as rays from some brilliant sun. The Israeli government had a strong champion in Einstein, and the original bust now reposes in the Chaim

Weitzman Institute in Palestine, although fortunately Jo made other copies of it, as he generally did of his best works.

The impression Einstein made on Jo was a lasting one. It had been an unusually enjoyable sitting and years later he spoke of it to Florence Lucius, his old friend of his student days, whom he was fortunate enough to meet again.

"It was so strange, Flossie," Jo commented, showing her the bust. "For it was almost freezing weather when I did this bust and when we went outside later, I noticed Doctor Einstein was nearly blue with the cold. But do you know, I don't even think he was aware of it? He didn't even wear socks!"

"Perhaps it surprised *you*, Jo," Flossie said in her merry, teasing manner, "but it shouldn't have. I've seen that same far-off expression in your face when you're concentrating on your work. And what's more, I have an idea that without your knowing it, Doctor Einstein must have wondered how you could be so hard at work without ever noticing your beard was splattered with ashes from your pipe!"

"Do I do *that?*" Jo was astonished.

But Flossie only nodded. She had always seen in Jo that same intensity and dreaminess as the man whose bust is one of his most superb works.

One day a charming mid-Western lady, Shannon Garst, visited the Claremore Memorial in Oklahoma. The memorial had been built in memory of an American cowboy, Will Rogers. Mrs. Garst was only one of the average thousand people per day who visit this memorial, and like them all, she was deeply affected by the experience. Unlike them, because she is a writer, it was not enough for her to merely talk about what she felt—she had to go home and write about it too. She called her book, *Will Rogers, Immortal Cowboy*. One of the things she said about her visit was:

"When I was in Claremore, Will Rogers' home town, I stared up at the heroic bronze statue of Will, trying to fathom the magic he possessed. His shrewd understanding eyes seemed to twinkle at mine and at that moment something happened to me. Then and there, I knew that more than anything else in the world I wanted to write Will Rogers' life story."

The story behind the Claremore Memorial is in many ways as much Jo's story as Will's. Both of them traveled extensively and met each other often. Jo had asked Will several times to sit for his bust, but Will always refused. He called Jo "An old head hunter." But that was Will. There were few things indeed about which he did not tease or joke. Both Will and Jo had met Mussolini, both had visited Russia, Will had flown with Charles A. Lindbergh, and Jo had sculptured the daring young pilot. They had seen and known many of the same things, and if Will had consented to sit for his bust, conversations probably would have been most exciting, but Will was reluctant and always put Jo off. To Jo, Will represented a brave symbol of all the freedoms America meant, especially freedom of speech. Why, Will often joked about the men who set world policies, even when they were sitting right in his audience! And, at the height of the depression, when people had more tears than laughter, Will could still make them grin.

Once, prior to the nomination of Franklin Delano Roosevelt for the presidency, there had even been talk about nominating Will! His comment on this was that he wouldn't run "no matter how bad the country will need a comedian by that time."

As the depression grew more severe, Will's wit still teased.

"We'll hold the distinction of being the only nation in the history of the world that ever went to the poorhouse in an automobile."

But for the most part the things he said were meant in fun. However, once he said something in his simple manner, so beautiful that few have ever said it better.

"I've joked about every prominent man of my time,

but I never met a man I didn't like. I'm proud of that. I can hardly wait to die so it can be carved on my tombstone."

In 1935, when Will was fifty-six, he and Wiley Post, who had already made a successful flight around the world in 1931 and established a record, decided to try for a new record. Tragically, the plane crashed in Alaska, shortly after it had taken off. Will and Wiley were both killed. The entire nation went into mourning.

The State of Oklahoma passed a bill to put up a statue of Will in Washington in National Statuary Hall, where each state is allowed to contribute bronze or marble statues of those whom she considers her two most distinguished citizens. Oklahoma had previously given Sequoyah, the great Indian chieftain, but she had bided her time, waiting for another man equally outstanding. Will Rogers was *that* man. When the announcement was formally made, Betty Rogers, Will's wife, asked that Jo be the sculptor. Betty and Will had been very close and she felt no one better understood how Will felt about people than did this sculptor whose feelings for them showed so plainly in all he did.

Jo asked for some of Will's old clothes. He also requested the Fox Film Company to let him have some of the popular Will Rogers' movies. When these things arrived in Jo's Paris studio, he got to work at once. He ran the films over and over again, watching Will's motions, his slow easy grin, how he sat and walked. As for the clothing, Jo believed the garments people wear retain the natural draping and form of the wearers. Certainly, Will's old clothes kept in them a tremendous amount of the physical Will.

At last Jo's plaster model of Will was finished, ready to be cast in bronze. By now it had been decided that there were to be two casts made. One would go to the National Gallery in Washington as intended. (Jo had already placed there in 1929 a fine statue of Senator LaFollette, selected by the people of Wisconsin. The ten years between the two statues showed a sculptor of even greater development.) As for the second cast of the model, this was to be placed in a handsome museum which had been built atop a hillside near Claremore, Oklahoma. Many years before, Will had bought this ground, hoping to build what he considered the ideal house. In a strange way, perhaps a pattern, he had achieved exactly what he might have wanted!

Nor did Jo forget the words Will wanted inscribed, for beneath Will's figure, on the base of the great bronze statue, is carved, "I never met a man I didn't like."

The inspiration people find at Claremore is no ac-

cident. Not only was Will outstanding, but this statue
of him, one of two major works Jo did in those last
years of the thirties, has in it a feeling so intense and
deep in understanding, that it touches the heart of the
beholder. Jo understood completely Betty's loss of
Will. Had he not lost Yvonne? Yet oddly, although Jo
didn't realize it, in that loss, something had happened
to him greater than his grief. Without Yvonne to give
to completely, as he always had, he now began to give
himself completely to his work. That is why in these
later works, there is not only the model, but part of
Jo himself.

Way back in 1925, Jo had entered in a competition
with ten other sculptors to do a statue of Walt Whitman, one of the greatest of American poets.

When he decided to enter the contest, Jo went
from library to library, from bookshop to bookshop,
reading everything he could find on Whitman—who
he was, where he came from, what he liked to do, how
he did it, and most of all, *why* he felt about things as
he did. At night, he would fall asleep with a book in
his hands, waking up in the morning to begin his reading all over again. He thought Whitman, ate Whitman,
slept Whitman! For all of that, he was nervous about
the contest. He had never thoroughly approved of
competitions, feeling they were bad for the contest-

ants. You could come so close to winning, so terribly close, and then—like that!—you lost. It was frightening. Besides, a contest didn't prove especially much anyhow. And yet, he did want to win. More than anything else he could think of, Jo wanted to be Walt Whitman's sculptor. You can imagine how thrilled he was when it was announced he had been chosen! How could anything possibly go wrong now?

Immediately, Jo plunged into making his plaster model of Whitman. He put into it all he believed Whitman meant and felt, working with such a fury of ambition that he was nearly exhausted. Then when he was finished, after all the plans, the months of hard work, the dreaming—it was for nothing. There wasn't any place for the statue to be erected!

Like my statue of the soldier, Jo thought. They had to put a street through my studio to make anything happen to it, and then look how it wound up. I don't think I can stand it again! But for all Jo's determination, the situation was hopeless. The original site had been found unsuitable, and although many other people desperately tried to find other places for the project, each one seemed to have some sort of restriction that made it impossible to place the figure there. This part of the park had too many statues already! Another part would certainly not show it to good advantage. Where could it go?

"Well," Jo said to his plaster model of Walt, "it isn't the first time for either of us, is it? You had your shares of ups-and-downs and I've had mine. We'll make out somehow!"

Jo never thought it strange that he talked to his model of Walt. In fact, the day he first began to work on it, he had talked to it and it had seemed exactly right.

"Camerado, I give you my hand. . . ."

No, it couldn't be! And yet, he could have sworn the figure answered him. Everytime he had done a good piece of sculpture, it always seemed to Jo it looked just about ready to speak out—as if the only thing missing in it was the voice. But with Whitman, there was much more. So very much more! Jo considered the statue he had made, the left hand held out as if in greeting. The figure was Walt Whitman walking, his strong stride ready to take in the dusty roads, the fields and hills of his country, the crowded city streets, loving the people—always the people. As for the face, it was eager, alive with delight in everyone and everything that was! How could anyone resist going along with a man such as Whitman? And yet here he was—confined to Jo's studio because there was no place in all his beloved outdoors where he might be placed!

Whitman was born in New York in 1819. In his

lifetime, his jobs included everything from wagon driver to fisherman. Wherever everyday people worked, Walt had a strong urge to work with them and become one with them.

The poetry Whitman wrote he wrote for these people. Poetry, however, is seldom a popular subject and Whitman wrote in a manner unlike anyone before him. He was trying to put into his words the rhythm of music and the language of common everyday speech. The people whom he loved didn't care particularly for his poetry, but how they loved him as a man! He was their friend and they knew it, and although they didn't always understand it, they were certain his poetry must be as strong and good as he was.

Whitman's beginnings were humble and he had known both poverty and homelessness. Yet he never felt humble or poor or homeless among people. For him, the common man was religion. Once he had written, "In the faces of men and women, I see God!" That alone would have been enough to make Jo Davidson want to do his statue. In the face of every man and woman Jo had ever looked upon, he had seen God. In doing Whitman, he felt as if he was really doing the heart part of himself.

One day an old friend of Jo's, Averell Harriman, later to be Governor of New York, visited Jo in his

Paris studio and was impressed by the plaster model of Whitman.

"Go on and admire it!" Jo told him. "This is probably as much of it as you or anyone else will ever see of it. I began plans on it darn near fourteen or fifteen years ago, and no one has ever found a place for it to stand!"

"I don't understand, Jo. Suppose you explain to me what happened."

And so Jo told Averell Harriman about the contest he had entered in the mid-twenties and here it was nearly the end of the thirties and Whitman was still in his studio.

Mr. Harriman was silent, thinking. Suddenly he snapped his fingers. "I've got a place for it, I think! How about Bear Mountain Park in New York?"

Jo stared at Mr. Harriman in confusion. He had had so many disappointments in his lifetime, and there was something about this particular statue—no, he didn't think he could take it if something went wrong again. Whitman had become such a part of him—closer than many of his friends, really!

"I—I'll have to know more about the place. It may not be exactly right. Perhaps Walt wouldn't have cared for it. It—well, how do I know what sort of place Bear Mountain is. . . . You do understand what I mean?"

Mr. Harriman laughed at Jo's protests. He was aware that Jo was quite serious about this particular piece of work, for Jo was never good at hiding his feelings. True, he had that huge beard and he never complained much, and yet in the dark eyes, in the strong features which rose above that handsome beard, there was an almost childlike honesty which no one could mistake.

"When you come home to America, Jo, you'll come and visit me. Then you can roam all over Bear Mountain Park and see for yourself if it isn't the one place in the world for Walt Whitman to stay!"

Averell Harriman was right. When Jo returned, he realized it for himself at once. Here was a fertile range of mountains so close to the sky one might reach up and try to pull down a cloud! There were paths leading through tall trees that seemed to point their branches up towards God and the silver ribbon of the Hudson River wound against the timeless rocks. Yes, this was the place where Walt belonged! Later, Jo learned that when Whitman had been alive he had often walked here. Eagerly now, Jo made his plans to have the plaster model cast so that it might be erected as soon as possible.

"Wonder if it's safe to visit Jo tonight," a friend might say. "He's so busy on his Whitman statue. Last time I visited him, I was Walt's right ankle! I'm be-

ginning to believe Jo doesn't look at anyone without
seeing some part of Whitman."

It was easy to believe that. From the first, Jo had
had people posing for Whitman. This one was his
arm, another his ears, but Jo was not upset if no one
showed up at all. Then he had time to talk to Whitman! He was quite convinced these days that Whitman continually answered him—not so anyone else
could hear, of course, but so that Jo couldn't possibly
not hear him. There was something unusual about this
statue that even he wondered over and over why he
should feel so differently about it. Why was it unlike
the rest? What was it about Whitman that disturbed
him so and yet made him so content?

"I don't understand it, Walt," he said, patting the
striking brow. "I don't think I've ever felt quite this
way before. One might think I'd lived with you and
did everything you did."

"New York was quite a different place when I was
a young man. But people stay the same. That's what
you feel, same as I. The people."

"Maybe, I don't know." Jo frowned, unconvinced.
He had always felt people, but this was different for
him, no matter what Walt said.

At last, the statue was unveiled at a public ceremony. When the veil dropped, Robert Moses, Com-
missioner of Parks for New York, made an altogether

astounding remark. He gazed at the statue curiously, then looked at Jo, then back at the statue. Finally he spoke to the people who had come to see the unveiling.

"I'm not sure," he said, "whether this is a statue of Walt Whitman by Jo Davidson or a statue of Jo Davidson by Walt Whitman!"

The people stared then too. First at the statue, then at Jo, then back at the statue, just as Mr. Moses had done. Then they nodded and laughed. Mr. Moses was right! Walt Whitman's statue looked as much like Jo outside as the hearts of both men must have resembled one another inside . . .

On a rock, opposite the statue, Jo had carved the words Walt had written—words he had often seemed to hear Walt say to him while he was working, "Camerado, I give you my hand. . . ."

Visitors at Bear Mountain Park, who go to see the statue of Whitman have taken those words to themselves. Walt's outstretched left hand is continually reached for and held by hundreds of people, so that now, that outstretched hand is worn and shiny.

Yet the strangest thing of all about it is that having taken that hand, clasping it tightly, warm in the sun, that strong bearded figure seeming so eager to be on his way, well—it's hard for a visitor to be really certain. . . .

Is it Walt's hand or Jo's hand that one holds?

Here, the chapter might have ended. Had not a place been found for the statue and Jo's heart made glad? But if there is genius, it is not for a day or a week or a year—in fact, it has no time limit. So that now, even though Jo is not here to see or know—or perhaps in a different way, a way of the spirit, he is—there is another place for Walt! Once again, that magnificent plaster mold will be cast and another eleven foot statue of Whitman will be placed on country both Walt and Jo knew well—the new Pennsylvania-New Jersey "Walt Whitman" bridge, spanning the busy Delaware River between Philadelphia and Gloucester.

And as the traveler passes the Whitman statues, wherever they may be, he shows a face in which either Walt or Jo could look and find God!

Those last years of the thirties, Jo worked so hard trying to forget his own personal sorrow and contributing generously to others who needed help, that he neglected his own well-being.

He saw Flossie fairly often these days and she always scolded him for overworking.

"Jo, you're doing too much. You can't keep on this way, working all hours of the day and night!"

But Jo didn't listen. Hadn't he always been strong

and well? Why worry? Besides, he had to keep on—
those gigantic statues of Will Rogers and Walt Whitman couldn't be done in a few hours. True, aside from
time, they took tremendous energy and strength, but
these are things any sculptor takes for granted, so what
of it?

What of it, indeed? One night in 1939, Jo found
out. He was having dinner with Flossie and some other
friends when suddenly he suffered an agonizing pain.
A few moments later, he collapsed and had to be
taken to the hospital. His doctor, Dana Atchley, cautioned him carefully.

"You've had a severe heart attack, Mr. Davidson.
From here on in, you're going to have to take things
easy. You can't possibly continue as you have!"

Jo understood. That dreadful pain, which had
traveled across his chest and down his left arm, seeming to squeeze his breath out of him, was not going to
be easy to forget. He felt horribly weak now, as if
that tremendous strength of his had left him completely. He realized that he was going to have to rest
for a long while, then think twice, or maybe even
three times, before plunging ahead with the heavy,
physical work sculpturing so often means. But resting
and taking things easy were strange to Jo. True, his
body might be safely bedded down, but his mind was
as active as ever and simply refused to stay quiet!

There was so much going on. Hitler had marched into Poland. Great Britain and France had announced war, and here he was, while all of this was going on— more history in the making—wasting his time in bed. It was really expecting far too much of him, bad heart or not!

He read a great deal and he worried even more. What was happening to his Paris studio? To his lovely country place in Becheron? By now, the Germans had probably taken them over, perhaps even destroyed all his busts and figures—the work of his lifetime! It was not a comforting thought.

Before he had been taken ill, he had visited his friends, Sam and Bella Spewack, the playwrights, at their farm in Bucks County, Pennsylvania. He found in the landlocked streams and pools, the rolling hills of this rich countryside, a strong resemblance to Becheron. The Spewacks had shown him a place nearby which was for sale. While he was ill, Jo asked an architect friend to look it over. The friend, Burrall Hoffman, liked the place and thought he could convert the barn into an excellent studio for Jo, although neither he nor anyone else really thought Jo would be doing much sculpturing from now on. Perhaps as a hobby or a place to putter. . . .

When he left the hospital, Jo went to the Virgin Islands to convalesce, but not before he had left definite orders to purchase the Bucks County farm. There was no way of knowing what German bombings had done to his French possessions—at least, he would still have a place to come home to now.

As Jo grew stronger, he took long walks, but they were walks that revealed more to him than the lush green scenery, the bright blue sky. He no longer played the game of "window shopping" as he had when he was a boy and a young man—he had no reason to. Life had been good to him and he had known much of what the world calls riches. Now, he did a different kind of thinking, and it disturbed him greatly for it was made up of memories. All kinds of memories, some good, some bad—but the trouble with each of them was that they represented the past. Didn't he have a future any more? Was life over for him now that he'd had an almost fatal heart attack? One day he rebelled! Mr. Hoffman had sent him a progress report on the new house. Things were coming along nicely. He was sure Jo would be pleased. Jo was sure of that too—Hoffman was extremely capable, but the important thing was that the place was getting done and that meant—most important of all—that there was a studio to work in. He made up his mind—no more memories, no more dreams of the past! He still had a future, no matter what anyone said. He had wasted enough time. There was work to be done. And as long as his heart held out, he would do it. He remembered the pain, the long days in the hospital and the long days afterwards of convalescing, but he remembered sculpturing too. If anything was going to happen to him, it would have to happen while he was working and that was all there was to it.

He had no idea how much time he had—nor did anyone else, but however long or short it would be, he was going to make the most of it.

11. The Forties

The world is a busy place in which things never seem to stop. For all of that, many things repeat themselves; wars, for instance. The forties saw World War II, the most destructive war the world has ever known. When Hitler came into power, there were nine million Jews in Europe. Before he had done, there were less than three million. . . .

The forties knew other events as well. By the end of the forties, a dream of thousands of Jews became a reality. May, 1948, became the official birthdate of a new nation, Israeli. Television was beginning to be as common in an American household as an automatic washing machine. The middle forties saw the sudden death of Franklin Delano Roosevelt, as well as the explosion of the first atomic bomb over Hiroshima. And the early forties saw the emergence of a great American general, who would later be President of the United States, Dwight David Eisenhower. A special award was given a young "pop" singer, Frank Sinatra for a song he sang about tolerance, "The House I Live In."

These people and events Jo knew and sculptured, the serious, the majestic, the seemingly trivial. Each in their own way, was history. The Germans might have destroyed what he had done in Paris and Becheron, but what of it? He had begun again. What was more, he would continue.

For a long time, Jo had been concerned with relations between North and South America. He felt particularly strongly on the subject now—in a world where war was an ever-present threat, the two Americas should stand firm together. One night at a gathering of some friends, he expressed his feelings.

"We're not doing enough! We must let our neighbors in South America know we are their friends and that we mean to stand together."

"And what do you suggest?" John Abbott asked with interest, for he was engaged in inter-American affairs and was gravely concerned about the situation.

"I'm not exactly certain, but I feel that perhaps we ought to send someone down who has a strong personality and no prejudices to convince these people that we are sincere in our gestures. I don't mean the standard brand of diplomat either!"

"But there are so many countries in South America," someone else pointed out. "Each of them is unlike the other. Neither their governments or their languages are identical. It's not an easy problem, no matter how good our intentions. We can't possibly send anyone but the most special diplomat we can find."

"That's all quite true." John Abbott agreed. "It would take an extraordinary personality to—" Suddenly he stopped talking and stared at Jo. An extraordinary personality! Was it not an extraordinary personality who had sculptured so many of the world's great men, so many different nationalities and ideas? So many different tongues and creeds? The rich and poor, peaceful and agitators, loved and hated—was it not indeed an extraordinary personality who had toured America, Europe, Asia, Africa, who could and did go anywhere and no matter where he went always seemed to belong?

The rest of the evening continued in a usual fashion, but every once in a while John Abbott would glance over at Jo and do a little more thinking.

The seed Jo had planted grew in fertile soil. John Abbott discussed it with Nelson Rockefeller, who was also seriously interested and concerned in the problem. A short while later, Mr. Rockefeller asked Jo to act as a special ambassador to South America! He was not only to represent all the good will and sincerity of an American visitor from the North, but he was to do a bust of each president of a South American country, as only Jo could.

Jo was at once delighted and upset. What a marvelous project! A terrific challenge. But was he well enough? He could ask the doctor, of course, although he thought he knew what the doctor would tell him. Was there enough time for him? For time had become a precious thing to Jo these days. He knew that it might easily run out on him—not that he was afraid, but he still had so much he wanted to do. Well, there was one way of saving time—that's what airplanes were for! He chuckled now recalling how he had once read about the Wright Brothers and their "experiment" and how he had wondered if he would ever be taking a ride in such a thing. But when he asked, Doctor Atchley said "No flying!" The South American countries boast some of the highest mountain areas in the world and flying over them in the rarefied atmosphere was definitely a bad thing for a heart patient.

Flying was not the only problem—there was one even more important. Jo needed an assistant if he was to take on this immense task. He thought most about this and he realized now that he didn't want just anyone. There was one special person for him, but would that *one special person* want him? How should he put it? Should he simply ask, "Flossie, will you take a chance on spending some of your precious hours with a sick, tired sculptor who hasn't too much time left of his own?"

Jo need not have worried, for Florence Lucius needed no words. From the day they had first met, she had always understood Jo's needs. And she understood how he felt about his work too, for she was an artist as well. And if time was so very valuable to Jo, no one more than Flossie knew what that meant too. During the years they were apart, Flossie had married someone else, rather unhappily, and what was worse she had had a darling youngster of her own, Boyce, whom she had lost when he was only ten. She remembered her son every day of his life and she was wise enough to know that she would not have exchanged one brief day of her child's existence for anything life could offer. Now she was willing to take a chance with Jo's time as well. If they were only meant to have a single day together, it would still mean something—*everything!* Flossie said an unconditional, enthusiastic "Yes" to Jo.

They made plans to be married at sea, for Jo wished to avoid as much publicity as possible. He was so famous that it was almost impossible for him to avoid publicity in anything. But the Dutch captain on whose ship they sailed was not permitted to marry anyone at sea, and so they were married in Venezuela in May, 1941.

As Jo had anticipated, despite the doctor's orders, if he was to make time, he would have to do some flying. From country to country—Brazil, Paraguay, Uruguay, Peru, Ecuador, Colombia, Bolivia, and others— he flew, modeling the presidents he met in clay, casting them in bronze on his return to the United States. There, they were exhibited at the National Gallery of Art in Washington. Later, they were given to the various countries as a gift from the United States.

It was a happy trip for Jo, a successful one too—not only for him, but for the two continents as well.

It had taken Jo six months to do the busts of eleven presidents in ten countries—a trip, which if he had had to follow transportation methods available in some of the more primitive of these lands, might have taken three or even four times as long.

"I wish," he told Flossie on their way home, "that I could have met the Wright Brothers and 'busted' them. Most of the credit for the success of our trip should be theirs."

"Not *most*, Jo. Certainly, no more than half. No one will ever convince me that the Wright Brothers could have done those busts as beautifully and rapidly as you did—or as 'W-right'!"

Jo laughed. It was always so much fun to be with Flossie, although the pun she had just made wasn't even good enough to serve with breakfast coffee and he told her so!

When they arrived back in New York, they were shown the many newspaper accounts of the trip. Reading them, it was easy to perceive that Jo Davidson had bettered North and South American relationships to an incredible degree.

While she was unpacking, Flossie turned to him. "How do you feel, Jo?"

"Fine, dear. A little tired. But I'll be ready for something else after I've had a good night's sleep."

"But you mustn't! You need a really good rest now.

Don't tell me you have another project in mind!" She saw Jo was grinning at her. "All right," she sighed, "but it had better not be too difficult."

"I haven't anything particular in mind right now, Flossie, but something will turn up. It always does."

"That's what I'm afraid of," Flossie said, wondering what he'd be doing next. With Jo, one could never tell.

Now Jo and Flossie settled down in Stone Court Farm, which is what he called his Bucks County home. He had a new assistant, Angelo Frudakis, who was obviously going to be a fine sculptor on his own one of these days, for Jo had an eye for capable young artists. There were always guests and good conversation, although much of the talk these days was of the war. What else was as important? Needless to say, Jo was much disturbed over what was going on—and as usual, he wanted to do something to help.

One day, Clifton Fadiman, the critic and writer, then working on the Writers' War Board, asked Jo to consider doing a memorial to portray the tragedy of Lidice.

Lidice had been a small village in Czechoslovakia, to which Hitler had sent one of his deputies, Reinhard Heydrich, known as "Heydrich the Hangman." Heydrich was to act as "Protector" of the country. The

Czechs had patterned their brave little nation, under the guidance of the remarkable Jan Masaryck and Eduard Benes, into a country as closely resembling the United States in ideas as they could make it. Heydrich made life intolerable for these people. Unable to bear his cruelty any longer, the Czechs assassinated him. In revenge, the Germans entered the little community of Lidice and destroyed the entire town, burning it. Then they killed every man among the five hundred townspeople, and sent the women and children into concentration camps. Hitler had said he destroyed Lidice so it would be forever wiped out in the memory of man. . . .

Jo sculptured a group representing a Lidice family. Flossie posed for the mother, the gardener's child was her youngster, and Angelo was the father. Jo depicted them as they might have looked only a moment before their destruction.

When the project was shown in the galleries of the Associated American Artists, people viewed it silently. So Hitler had destroyed Lidice! Well, Jo Davidson had re-created it as a lasting testimony which would never be forgotten.

And now in the forties, Jo and Flossie met a human "miracle!"

Over and over again, all our lives, we keep hearing about miracles. Few of us ever see what we really know is a miracle. Even fewer have any idea about such things at all.

For people of other religions, there are shrines where it has been said that the blind suddenly receive sight and the crippled learn to walk. Thousands of people travel huge distances to such places, hoping for a cure of whatever ailment they may have. Yet thousands more, with the same ailments, are seen everyday in hospitals, where miracles of precisely the same kind take place and are taken for granted, because they are performed by doctors. Some people respond to religious statues, others to trained scientists. And so we know that these so-called "miracles" rest not with the sick, not with the shrine or hospital, but with God and God alone—and always in His time and place.

But what of the blind who do not regain sight? Or the crippled who never walk? What of the hundreds of people, born with parts of their bodies missing, who never grow a new arm or leg or begin to hear or see in shrine or hospital? Is there then no "miracle" for them? *Or does the miracle exist all the same though we may not recognize it?*

In the Bible, we are told many times of miracles,

but they always seem to have been done by God for the doubting—those who had enough faith never needed these things.

In the small town of Tuscumbia, Alabama, in 1880, a little girl, Helen Keller, was born. She was a delightful baby, and until she was nineteen months of age, she did all the wonderful things babies do to make them adored. She learned to make sounds, not too clear to be sure, for they were infant sounds for infant thoughts and she was a normal baby. Then a sudden vicious disease, affecting the brain and spinal cord, struck her and she awoke one morning to a world where the bright eyes of her infancy saw nothing and the fragile flowers God gives babies for ears heard nothing. Sight and sound had left her forever! For the rest of her life, she would live in a world of darkness and silence. She was still a beautiful baby, but a baby for whom the world had no meaning or any way of reaching her. Who could make themselves known to such a child? Who could give her a way to see and hear?

Jo met Helen Keller at a party in 1942. At that time, the world was once more adding to Helen's difficulties. People had said it before and were saying it again—she was a pretender and really could see and hear!

"No one can tell me she can't see!" someone would say. "There was that bowl on the dinner table, full of pink, white, and red roses, yet she picked out just a few and said 'What lovely *pink* roses!' She *must* have seen!"

"If someone spelled things into my hands the way that companion of hers, Polly Thompson, does, I'd never be able to get it that fast unless I'd already heard it or seen the speaker's lips."

Jo and Flossie heard all the gossip. As always, they waited to see for themselves.

"A hyacinth is a hyacinth!" someone standing nearby said in a loud tone. "I don't believe for a second Helen Keller can tell a white one from a purple one!"

"Sounds like Gertrude Stein's 'Rose is a rose' business," Jo remarked to Flossie.

"I wonder," Flossie said curiously, "what Helen Keller would make of Gertrude Stein."

"I don't know, but from what we've heard, maybe Gertrude's sentence would never have been written!"

Because he had always been interested in people and nothing was too much trouble for him if it meant reaching through to someone else, Jo had taken time years before to learn the manual method of talking to a deaf person. Now when he met her, Jo could talk

directly into Helen's hand! Other people could doubt
Helen's abilities all they wanted to—Jo knew the
truth.

Helen and Jo became good friends immediately.
Here was someone with whom she could speak directly. True, Polly Thompson, hour after hour, day
after day, held her hand, staying with her, her love
and concern spelling into Helen's hand all that was
going on about her. Before Polly, there had been Hel-
en's untiring teacher, Anne Macy Sullivan, who had
taught Helen everything she knew, but like Polly was
only able to direct or respond to the shining spirit inside Helen. There had been others to help too. All
over the world, people of all kinds, men and women in
whom God's goodness gleamed like a star in the black-
ness of Helen's night, had helped. Now the rays
which Jo sent out to her came through strong and
bright. From the beginning, Helen spoke of the amazing "life force" she felt in Jo. Later, Jo taught Flossie
how to speak to Helen too and soon all four of them,
Jo and Flossie, Helen and Polly, were close friends.

On the way home the night of the party, Jo was
unusually silent and Flossie knew he was deep in
thought. He often had such moments. People could
move about him, laughing, even photographing him
as he worked, rattling cups or glasses, and Jo continued as if none of them was there. Nothing existed

for him then but the life he was trying to bring
through his clay! He could joke or comment and then
suddenly—snap! It was gone and the handsome face
grew serious, the dark eyes intense—almost aglow
with strange fire, and Jo Davidson was in a world of
his own. Flossie always respected these silences.

"He's at home with his soul," she'd tell herself,
"and he's put up a 'Do not disturb' sign on the door of
his brain."

Patiently she would wait then for the return of the
gentle, amusing man she loved so much.

They were just turning out the lights, getting ready
for bed, when Jo turned and said, "Could we have
Helen and Polly come and stay with us for a while?
I'd like to do her bust!"

Now it was Flossie's turn to be silent. What would
it be like to have someone in the house who was blind
and couldn't hear? If the furniture should be moved
and a chair not put back in the same place, there could
be an accident. And there were always so many people visiting, coming to see Jo, it often seemed to
Flossie that nothing was in order. How about meals?
How did Helen Keller manage about those?

"There isn't any truth in what people are saying, is
there, Jo? I mean about Helen's being able to see and
hear? She can't really, can she?"

"No, it's not true. Someday people may talk about

me too and who knows what they'll say? It may be equally untrue, and yet they'll believe it! I only hope I have Helen's courage and that I learn to bear it without complaint or explanation. And," he lifted his head proudly, "I hope too there will always be someone who can see the truth as easily for me as I saw it for Helen tonight."

A short time later Helen and Polly came to Stone Court Farm to visit with Jo and Flossie. There were no accidents. Helen stepped around things as if she had been there in the house all her life. She touched silverware and china at the table to find out where each piece was before using it. She spilled nothing. She told Luigi, the gardener, which lilacs were white and which were lavender. She talked to Angelo Frudakis, running her sensitive fingers quickly over his face and torso and told him exactly how he looked.

"She makes me ashamed," Angelo told Flossie. "I can see and hear, yet she sees and hears more than I ever have or will!"

"Helen proves we have many more senses than the five we were taught about in school," Flossie said, understandingly.

Angelo nodded. He knew that living with Jo was a special experience and that in just a few months he had learned much never covered in any art class. He was more interested in the technique of his art than

Jo was, but he realized that Jo's immense feeling for people had about it a kind of seeing few other people ever had and that because of it his work would never be like anyone else's—anymore than Helen Keller's mind would ever be like anyone else's. Both of them had a kind of sight, an inner sense, that nothing could quite explain!

When Jo finished Helen's bust, he was dissatisfied with it. Helen was elated. She went over and over her own features, her perceptive fingers tracing the eyes, nose, the mouth she had never seen. She had already gone over dozens and dozens of other heads in Jo's studio, identifying each by touch. Some she had met in person and her fingers remembered for her what she could not see.

"Gandhi," she'd say. "Einstein. George Bernard Shaw." She made no mistakes, her hands as certain in their way as Jo's in his.

"She's beautiful!" Angelo said. "And it shines out of her, yet there is something about that bust—"

"Yes?" Jo said with his ever-open mind.

"Well, somehow that bust doesn't seem complete! Helen Keller needs something more in her bust than just her face." Abruptly, Angelo was embarrassed. What right had he to make such a suggestion to Jo Davidson of all people—Jo who always understood and felt things about people so keenly?

"But you're absolutely right, Angelo! Why didn't I think of it? It's Helen's hands I've missed! They're so important too—how could I have slipped up like that. I must be getting old!"

Old, Angelo thought! Jo Davidson *old?* He's young as a bud. And his humility—as if people were doing him a favor when they make a suggestion, especially when the suggestion means days and nights of doing a job all over again.

"You don't mind? After all—you *are* the boss!"

"And what good is a boss who can't learn anything more? The day we stop learning from others is the day we stop growing!"

And so, once more Helen Keller was "busted," this time her hands upraised in one of her typical gestures, her face strong and sweet in an expression of inner beauty.

Many people have seen both busts. Some have been disturbed by them. It is perhaps because these busts are unlike anything Jo did, but there is again an extremely good reason why.

When one is without sight and hearing, then one is capable of having none of the fears most people have. Helen's whole life reveals this.

When she was a young girl, she learned all about the animals people have around their homes and farms; sheep, cows, horses, many kinds of dogs (some of

whom were her own pets). There were also trips to
the zoo, where Helen put her hands in the lion's
mouth and down his body. She even allowed snakes to
crawl around her! Gently, she felt giraffe and ele-
phant, zebras, birds, dozens of other beasts which most
people who can see and hear merely stare at through
bars.

She had traveled all over the world, touching the
well and the sick, some ill with diseases the seeing
world completely avoided. She had touched the un-
fortunate victims of wars at the very site of their
wounds! She felt people with her hands—regardless of
color and creed. Like Jo, who could see and hear, she
loved them solely for being what they were—people.

There was perhaps only one person of all those
whom she met who had ever rejected her. That was
George Bernard Shaw, the playwright. Later he de-
nied that having Helen touch him had upset him. His
excuse was that he found it "embarrassing." Nothing
so clearly reveals what Shaw was *not* and Helen *was*
as that small incident, just as Jo's own bust of Shaw
shows him possessed of greatness stained with more
than a little of the vain, the envious, and the wicked.
(No wonder Shaw preferred the head Rodin had done
of him which he thought made him resemble Jesus!)

So because Helen lived in a world where fear and
hatred, which may often be the *same* thing, could not

enter, her face revealed trust and sweetness, as few humans possess them. It was almost as if she had no exterior parts at all so that Jo did not have to "catch" her from within—her complete soul was plain to be seen by everyone who ever met her! And that is why Helen Keller is as much of a "miracle" as any we are ever likely to encounter.

Jo introduced Helen to an old friend of his, Van Wyck Brooks, one of the most learned and honest American writers of our times. Van Wyck lived in Connecticut, as Helen and Polly did. Soon he too became a close friend of Helen's, writing a simple and superb book about her called *Helen Keller, Sketch for a Portrait*. The sketch is as complete a picture of Helen as Jo's bust is. Brooks found in Helen what Jo too had seen.

Sometimes Van Wyck and Helen would talk about Jo and Helen would say Jo was one of the few people in the world in whom she had felt the "life force" so strongly. Flossie too exchanged letters and visits with them. Once Van Wyck wrote Flossie about Jo, saying, "He's an entire United Nations in his own way" and so of course he was!

L·E·F·

12. Jo Stands Firm

Almost every Jewish ceremony teaches us that both
gladness and bitterness are a part of life. And each
decade Jo lived, he learned that this was so—for each
decade brought him both joy and sorrow.

One night, in the middle forties, Jo was sitting with

a friend, Robert Flaherty, the father of the documentary film. Jo had once made a fine bust of him. They were talking, as they often did, about the ordinary "garden variety" of people, in whom both of them firmly believed.

The telephone rang and Jo rose to answer it. The caller, representing a New York shop, asked if Jo would lend for display the bust he had made of President Roosevelt. Jo inquired the reason for such sudden interest and so learned the grievous news, which by now everyone else seemed to have heard from an interrupted broadcast. Franklin Delano Roosevelt had died!

Jo and Flaherty sat silently together then, their thoughts having no need for words. Jo remembered the two inaugural medals he had done for Roosevelt, the thrill which he had known when he saw the crippled President and the blind-deaf Helen Keller shake hands across the bridge of triumph each of them had built of their lives. He remembered how when he had made the last medal, he had had to work unusually fast and couldn't quite see as well as he would have liked—it was most important to have the light fall just the right way on the President's profile. He kept shifting from place to place. After all, Roosevelt had all he could do to sit, let alone stand and move about to suit a sculptor. When Jo finished, the

President reached over, picked up a nearby book and wrote in it, "To Jo Davidson, in search of light." As in most things the President did, the inscription had a far deeper meaning and Jo understood that completely.

The war years brought many people to America and Jo sculptured many of them. One was Madame Chiang Kai-shek, whose husband, General Chiang Kai-shek, was leader of the Chinese Republic forces.

He also did Ernie Pyle, beloved newspaper reporter, who wrote his columns even as he lay next to the wounded and dead on the battlefields and who died as he would have wished—in their midst.

He did any number of important leaders and an outstanding general, Dwight D. Eisenhower. Eisenhower's outstanding characteristic was his determination to be fair at all costs. He always listened to both sides of an argument. It was this trait in him that Jo sensed most sharply and Jo was one who knew only too well how difficult it is to achieve such fairness. Eisenhower had a keen sense of humor and he and Jo exchanged jokes continuously through the sittings. In fact, Jo "caught" Eisenhower, just as his lips were about to break into laughter.

Though Roosevelt represented ideas altogether different from those of "Ike" and Jo had deeply revered Roosevelt as a friend, he worked just as hard on Eisenhower's bust as he had on Roosevelt's. He felt in this man a sense of fair play that deserved an equal amount in return!

After the war was over, Jo was approached and asked to erect a memorial in tribute to the millions of Jews Hitler had slaughtered in the Warsaw Ghetto. The memorial was to be erected in New York, and it was through Jo's efforts and the understanding and assistance of Robert Moses that a fine site was found for it. Then the project fell through and Jo's hopes were destroyed—not because Jo failed to do his part, nor yet because he wasn't right about what the memorial should be.

When he had been asked to do the memorial, he decided to research it thoroughly—as he had Whitman. Know everything there was to know about it. Breathe it, eat it, sleep it! Make it become part of him so that there was nothing about it he did not understand or feel.

He made a trip to Poland to see what Hitler had done—he had to see it all for himself. And he wrote in his autobiography, "I felt the Warsaw Ghetto story as a personal tragedy, not only because those involved were Jews, but because they were human beings, and people had always been my concern."

Jo went over the photographs of what Warsaw had

been *before* Adolph Hitler, what it had become *during* Adolph Hitler, what it was like *after* Adolph Hitler. Everything he saw aroused anguish and pity in him.

With the help of Ely Jacques Kahn, Jo drew sketches of what he thought the memorial should be —the history of the people. Was it not the history of the people which Moses recorded in the first five books of the Bible? Are not the Jews themselves *the people of history?*

One of Jo's plans was to show a mother, her dead child in her arms, killed by the Nazis. Another was to reveal an old couple, all the love and labor of their years together about to be murdered in the gas chambers by the hatred of the monster, Hitler. The project was made up of such things as these—all the afflictions which the people of the Warsaw Ghetto had endured. Like the many afflictions Pharaoh set upon the Jews in Egypt! So Jo wanted to cry out in stone the story of the horrors Hitler had visisted upon the people, yet they endured. This was what Jo believed was the true meaning of the Warsaw tragedy. The committee which had asked Jo to do the project had other ideas.

They wanted a memorial which would show a menorah and a star of David and other symbols of ritual. Jo knew that the main thing about all Jews is their belief in *one* God as a whole people, as Moses found them, and set them free. Father Abraham had no symbols when he first knew God. After the temple was destroyed and all the holy vessels with it, the Jews had no symbols. And if every Jewish symbol in the world were destroyed tomorrow morning at five o'clock, the Jews would still endure!

"The only thing that matters," Jo argued, "is that we matter to God as people!"

His feeling about this was so firm, so deep, that he could do the project no other way. The committee stuck to its own ideas. Plans for the memorial failed completely.

It might have been a beautiful monument that all the world could have looked on and understood, if Jo had been allowed to go ahead—just as the Old Testament is a book for all the people and not merely a few.

Still, the plans are all drawn and who knows—perhaps someday, in God's own time, the memorial may yet be built.

And while all this was going on, in another part of the globe, a small country celebrated its first birthday, which was strangely enough a memorial to the Jews of the Warsaw Ghetto too. History was being made in Israel. And where history was being made, Jo Davidson went!

Jo had "lost time" in the forties; once when he had traveled to San Francisco for the opening of the United Nations, and once for the trip to Warsaw. Both of them had been far too much for his over-taxed heart. He arrived in San Francisco only to spend his entire stay there in the hospital! When he was able to be up and about those first few days, his nurse, Julie Wilson, told Flossie a curious thing.

"We went out to the park," she said. "The same place I always take the heart patients to walk. It's so relaxing and quiet there and there are benches to sit on if a patient gets tired." As she spoke, her face had an unusual pallor—it was as if she was trying to tell something she wasn't quite sure she had seen and yet she had.

"Well?" Flossie prompted her gently. "Did Jo overdo it?"

"Oh no, Mrs. Davidson! Nothing like that. He was very good and took it easy—as he's supposed to do. Then I thought we ought to sit down and rest and we did—and that's when it happened."

"What happened? I don't understand."

"I'm not sure if I do either. That's why it's so hard to tell about. You see, it's a regular little park—the kind you have in any city—some old trees, a bit of grass, lots of squirrels and pigeons. And usually, there are the same people there, people who go every day. The birds and squirrels get to know them and come right over because they generally have something to feed them. Peanuts or corn or whatever it is they generally eat." Julie Wilson stopped and shook her head. "They *know* those people. They're there all the time. That's why I don't understand this. I've never been to that park before and seen anything like it and I've been with dozens of other patients."

Flossie was still. She realized that whatever had disturbed Julie Wilson was something she would have to explain in her own way. In a moment or so, Julie went on.

"You see, Mrs. Davidson, the pigeons and squirrels all left those regular people who come every day. They left them and came over to Mr. Davidson and sat on his shoulders and his lap and anywhere else they could be close to him! And they stayed. I've never seen anything before like that!"

"Animals have always liked Jo," Flossie said quietly. "We always have pets at home and I guess other animals know he likes them too."

"But the other people are just as fond of them and have something to feed them besides! Maybe I'm not explaining this well, Mrs. Davidson, but I know what I saw. And I know I never before saw it with anyone else in my whole life. There's something ex-

tremely special about your husband and the animals
know it too. And that's why they came!"

Afterward, Flossie asked Jo what kind of a day he
had had. He told her it had been lovely, that he
felt much better, and he was sure he was getting
stronger. Flossie prodded a bit, asking about the animals. He told her how friendly they had been and
said Julie Wilson had thought it was a little odd.

"But you don't, do you, Jo?"

"Why no. They're tame animals. They probably
sense that I'm a tame animal too."

"Oh, Jo! Don't you ever stop joking?"

All the same, neither Julie nor Flossie was ever altogether sure that there hadn't been something most
unusual. Years later, fatally ill, Julie called out for
Flossie, wanting to talk about it all over again. She
was certain she had seen something quite special—
something unforgettably wonderful. Perhaps it was
the same thing Helen Keller had sensed in Jo—that
"life force"! Had the animals felt it too?

Those last years of the forties, Jo tried to take it
easy. He missed doing all the work he had hoped to
do at the United Nations Conference, and the Warsaw
Ghetto arguments had made him ill too. But as 1950
came along, he felt much more the way he used to,
ready and eager for work. When an invitation came

to his Paris studio to travel to Israeli and see what was going on there, he was at once full of plans. Flossie had all she could do to restrain him.

"Please, Jo, you must remember! You've got to take it easy. We'll go and you can look around, but don't dare overdo it."

Even as she said it, Flossie knew it was useless. Jo was so enthusiastic over being able to go to Israel and see what was going on for himself. She looked at him and shook her head. His beard was almost white, but his eyes still sparkled like the eyes of the young boy she had first known. His humor was sharp, his joyousness unbounded. How could anyone or anything hold him down?

Jo came back from his Palestine trip the middle of December, 1951, thoroughly exhausted. So much had happened. So many changes!

Far away, across the Pacific, the first hydrogen bomb had been exploded at Eniwetok. The United Nations Building in New York was nearly completed. Jo's good friends, André Gide, the writer, and Robert Flaherty had both died. And Sinclair Lewis. Somehow it was hard to think about death when so much life was going on in the marvelous country from which he had just returned. Life was so exciting and now he had plans for a wonderful new project! Everyone he had met in Israel had been interested in it too. It would cost a tremendous amount of money, of course, and sculpture is always a luxury, but what of it? Somehow, he would get other people who could help interested in the project and what had been a little idea would become an outstanding place to visit and see the wonders of Israel in the making!

"It will take so much money to do what you have in mind, Jo." Flossie was thoughtful. "And somehow or other, I don't think it's anything someone else can do for you."

"A one-man project, you think? Well, perhaps you're right, Flossie. But Israel is full of one-man projects, each of them working together to make a new kind of nation."

He was quiet then, remembering. It was almost the same kind of world into which he had been born, when America was finding her way and men like Buffalo Bill were roaming the vast plains. Out of such greatness, America had risen. Surely out of this new venture, Israel would do the same. And this time—he would be right there to see it happen! History in the making. It fascinated him. He would do busts and statues of all the leaders of Israel so that everyone, everywhere, would be able to see exactly what these people were like, the strength and courage that promised that glorious future showing in every line of their

faces. Not flat, like a painting, but in three dimensions
—to walk around, to feel, to be as near the real thing
—*inside* and out—as was possible.

"Next year," he told Helen Keller, "we'll all go
together. There's no place like it! A rugged scrap of a
land and everyone working like fury to make it succeed."

"Of course, Jo. I can hardly wait to see it all!"

"Nor can I!" He snapped his fingers. "Why now
that I think of it, the time is too far off. It's practically
the first of January now. Nineteen fifty-two! We
won't wait a moment beyond early spring to go."

"Jo," Flossie pleaded, "you need to rest."

"I'm fine! Just fine, Flossie. A little tired, but by
spring, I'll be ready again. Wait and see."

That last week in December, the days crawled for
Jo. He returned to Becheron for a few days rest.
There, he tried to relax as much as possible, but he
kept thinking about all the work he intended to do
on his return to Israel. He sketched some of the
plans he had in mind for the project; the original
idea had already been approved. This time, next year
—God willing—perhaps the project would be nearly
finished!

He thought of some of the things he had done during this short visit. The head of Chaim Weizmann,
the first President of Israel. The unafraid-of-anything-

valor in the head of David Ben Gurion. Golda Meir,
ex-school teacher from America, first Labor Minister.
And that other woman too, Miriam Baratz, a true
pioneer—her chin firm, steady, the chin of a good
soldier. Yet her cheeks had been soft and curving,
the cheeks of a gentlewoman. What citizens these
people were! So many different nationalities! Yet
their brotherhood had made them one under *one* God.
And there were still so many, many Israelis to be
"busted." Heads of determined, fearless men and
women who believed in building a clean, new nation
out of nothing but hope, courage, and a soil that
brains and hard work made fertile. How could he
possibly wait to go back? If only he didn't feel so
tired. So awfully tired. He had said early fall, but he
would try to make it by spring. Funny, right now,
how far away spring seemed.

He remembered the sketch he had made of a young
woman he had watched helping to make a road. She
was the mother of four children, and here she was
building a road! Once she had been a teacher. Now
she worked on a highway. And she saw nothing unusual about it.

"This is a way of teaching too," she had told him.
"I make a road so the children can travel it to the
fine schools someone else is building at the end of
the road."

And the dark handsome face of the young tailor in Tel Aviv, who played first violin there in the Symphony Orchestra at night.

"We're all doing our part to help," he explained to Jo. "At night, I play music to give my people beauty and comfort. During the day, I mend their clothes. None of us can work without one another, but together—together we can build a nation."

If only I were younger, Jo thought, I'd go right off and work beside them. I'd sculpture for them at night and during the day I'd help build. I haven't such strong muscles in my arms and such a powerful chest for nothing. I could do it all right. Haven't I always been a good worker—sure and fast? Still, right now, I'm a bit tired. Too much traveling. Would tire out anyone. Better rest awhile, then I'll be all right. Able to go ahead. Be able to do everything, once I'm rested. Must stay a long while next time. Such a terrific amount of work to do. Only right now, better sleep. So tired. . . .

The New Year came and went. January first, nineteen fifty-two. Jo slept right through it in a little hospital outside Becheron. Slept right into January second, nineteen fifty-two, still dreaming his last dreams.

And finally, on that last day—that second day of a

new year, a new history in the making, Jo slipped quietly into eternity. The tired muscles relaxed, the great heart inside the huge chest cage stopped its weary beating, the wondrous hands fell to his side. Now at last, Jo Davidson was one with God.

Covenant Books

*Stories of Jewish Men and Women
To Inspire and Instruct Young People*

Covenant Books are a new and fascinating series designed to take young people, eleven to fifteen years of age, on an adventurous expedition into the realms of Jewish experience. This is achieved by means of colorful biographies of Jewish personalities—prophets, rabbis, martyrs, philanthropists, writers, scientists—each representative of the many facets of a great tradition. Interestingly written, with a wealth of background information, Covenant Books will stimulate the young reader's interest in his cultural heritage and prove a rewarding spiritual experience.

SILVERSMITH OF OLD NEW YORK: MYER MYERS *by William Wise.* A dramatic story of old New York and of the ambitions and struggles of one of the first great Jewish artists and patriots of Colonial Times.

BORDER HAWK: AUGUST BONDI *by Lloyd Alexander.* The story of an immigrant from Vienna in 1849, who found opportunities for continuing his idealistic struggles for freedom in his new home as he had struggled in the old.

JUBAL AND THE PROPHET *by Frieda Clark Hyman.* The story of the son of an important priest in the First Temple; of the prophet Jeremiah during the time that Jerusalem is under siege by the Babylonian army.